Advance Praise for
Saying Inshallah with Chutzpah

"In a world of increasing division and hatred, this inspiring book holds out a vision and hope for human renewal and reconciliation."
—Rabbi Paul Citrin, author of *I Am My Prayer: A Memoir and Guide for Jews and Seekers*

"Jessica Keith has just the kind of fresh and funny voice that our country needs right now. Timely, sardonic, and insightful, Keith speaks to the heart of cultural questions of belonging, acceptance of what it means to know a person beyond a cultural label. Hilarious and eye-opening!"
—Marni Freedman, author of *Permission to Roar*

"This thoughtful work offers us a model for resilience, while illustrating the best of humanity through humor and other powerful cultural synergies."
—Rabbi Jason Nevarez, Congregation Beth Israel, San Diego, California

"Jessica Keith is a rare voice—one that combines extraordinary sensitivity, deep understanding, expansive curiosity, and genuine authenticity. Hers is a voice to which we should give ear—she expresses a vision of what real human connection ought to look like in our broken and fractured world."
—Rabbi Dan Levin, Temple Beth El, Boca Raton, Florida

D1452101

SAYING
Inshallah
WITH
Chutzpah

A Gefilte Fish Out of Water Story

JESSICA NAOMI KEITH

A POST HILL PRESS BOOK
ISBN: 979-8-88845-100-7
ISBN (eBook): 979-8-88845-101-4

Cover design by Conroy Accord

Post Hill Press
New York • Nashville
posthillpress.com

Published in the United States of America
1 2 3 4 5 6 7 8 9 10

Thank you to my crew who light my fire and lift me up—
only with you by my side can I even dream of flying.

Contents

Chapter 1

Sailing In Uncharted Seas

"You're marrying a Black man, right?" Hala, the front desk receptionist, asked, passing out the morning mail. The middle-aged Arab divorcée, who winked at men with her head uncovered, let the words fall so naturally out of her mouth, I nearly forgot *I* was the foreigner. "He'll get you pregnant right away!" she said with a thrill in her tone and a punch of her fist in the air. "I know cause my daughter married a Mexican, and they are the same way."

Eating pomegranate seeds for my morning snack, my mouth was full, keeping me from using the words I was at a loss for anyway. The sweet seeds, soured by the indignation, now tasted of bile burning my throat. To avoid staining my clothes bloodred, I used more caution with my movement than Hala used with her words. She took a deep breath through her nose as if to try to smell if I was in heat. The pomegranate, a sign of fertility, rested in the palm of my hand.

In July 2009, I worked as an academic advisor in Los Angeles, California, on the eighteenth floor of the famous Century City twin towers. The highly acclaimed business complex resembled the designer's previous work, the World Trade Center.

I walked down the corridor of our office suite, the silver color of my wrap dress barely peeking through the oversized full-length knit sweater that covered my body like a blanket. The walls were decorated with the framed faces of the Kuwaiti royal family, their gazes as skeptical as my thoughts—perhaps all of us wondering how I, a thirty-one-year-old Jewish woman, was working at the Consulate of Kuwait, a sheep in wolf's clothing. The bottom corner of every picture, stamped with a crest, an emblem of a sailboat, reminded me I was in uncharted waters. A few months ago, I would not have been able to find the country on a map. And here I stood, employed by a Muslim government, planning my Jewish wedding, with the knowledge that Jews were not allowed to work here.

I dragged my heels in the hallway, delaying the dreaded swarms of advisors circling the cultural attaché for his signature on every government request. I, however, needed the official crest stamped in red ink to approve time off for my impending nuptials. Nubia, a middle-aged Egyptian divorcée, who deciphered what she wanted to as the Arabic translator, stormed out of Dr. Mohammad's office, the first in command.

"*Khalas*. Enough," she yelled, frustrated that her loose translations were not getting the message across.

I froze, staring at the boat, pretending I had not heard the yelling, directing my eyes to look captivated by the picture that I walked by fifty-seven times a day. In my effort to seem oblivious, I had not noticed Nubia on approach, now standing inches away from my body. Hissing sharply by my ear, "*Habibti*, I warn you. The winds do not always blow as the vessels wish."

Six months before my wedding date, I moved 120 miles away from my fiancé as a last-ditch effort to see if I could make it on my own. The decision proved to be as questionable as my sanity. Now with only three months till the big day, my to-do list included sending out invitations and getting the Kuwaiti crest stamped on my vacation request form, both higher on my list of priorities than buying a wedding dress.

I held the form in my hand, looming like the thought in my head that walking down an aisle was an act for an audience. So many obstacles stood in the way of taking this next step, from moving forward in life. At the time, it had not dawned on me what Dr. Mohammad meant when he said, "Entering the bath is not the same thing as leaving it." Feeling like I was drowning in work and life, I took a deep breath as I tread carefully into his office.

"You know, no one's allowed vacation until they've been here six months," Nahla, a twenty-something coworker who looked forty and dressed head-to-toe in Ralph Lauren, interrupted my thoughts. Minding everybody's business but her own, she chimed in after noticing the form in my hand.

I don't need your approval, I thought, agitated by her attempt to interfere.

Dr. Mohammad glanced at the form and then looked back at his phone and, while texting away, said, "Marrying one woman is like eating chicken every day for the rest of your life."

"I like chicken," I was surprised to hear myself say.

I moved the form towards Dr. Mohammad, knowing he loved weddings—just not those of his employees. "You know, Jessica Keith," Dr. Mohammad said with a giant grin. "Always look and smell like a flower," he continued in a sweet tone and then lowered his voice, "or your husband will want to smell other flowers."

Not giving him another moment to pause, I pushed the form under his pen, forcing his hand to sign.

"Anything else, Dr. Mohammad?" I said in a polite tone, hoping this one time something would be left unsaid.

"You know…" Dr. Mohammad paused, ensuring my undivided attention, "Seriously, it's sweet. Tyrone has just you."

I squinted my eyes, trying to translate his message. "You know what we say?" He paused to see if I agreed, "More wives, more problems."

Six Months Earlier

I sat in the passenger seat as we headed to the job interview, while my friend Leah took the wheel. She spent the day doing a mitzvah, a good deed, and a huge favor, driving me from San Diego to LA. Her fluorescent pink-polished nails tapped to the beat of the drum humming from the radio, unmoved by the traffic that forced me to double down on beta-blockers to obstruct my view. A 5'10" frame dressed in cutoff jean shorts and a tank top hanging by a thread and showing off her barely there tan lines. With the windows rolled down, her long blonde hair flowed as free as her spirit and as loose as her bra strap. A black business suit weighed me down, covering the drips of a meltdown between my back and a white blouse. I panted with my head directed out the window, the air conditioning vents facing my direction, set on high, to keep my sweat from leaving a mark.

Dropping me off in front of an office building with the address of the interview, which blended into the background of a concrete jungle, Leah said, "I'll be at the mall."

Large black sunglasses covered my eyes, keeping the bright sun from shining a light on the discreet entrance door. The glasses slipped to the middle of my nose, allowing my eyes to adjust. A dark hallway led to an empty waiting room revealing as much as the job posting on craigslist. "Positions Available. Kuwait Cultural Office. Location in LA TBD." In December of 2008, the United States was amidst an economic disaster with banks needing bailouts, and layoffs swept the nation. The few unbroken fluorescent lights offered a glimpse of the dimly lit space, where I sat alone, seeing it as an opportunity.

"Enter through the side door," a woman's voice echoed from an intercom, bouncing off the walls throughout the empty room. Six months into the job hunt, temp work was all I could find, and I was barely earning enough to afford the gas to get to this interview. The sedatives worked against me, causing my thoughts to be stoic, yet, the moment I heard the buzz unlocking the secured door, I pushed forward.

On the other side, the office assistant introduced herself, "I'm Hala." *Challah? Like the Jewish bread?* I wondered. She walked in front of me, writing notes on her bright yellow legal pad, mumbling to herself. At the only occupied office, she put her hand out, directing me to walk in first towards the man in the room yelling in Arabic. His full name on the email signature he sent with the address for the interview said Dr. Mohammad a h h a f aa f Al Harbi. "That's Dr. Mo," Hala introduced the diplomat and cultural attaché for Kuwait. His height, at over six feet tall, mirrored his high-ranking position. Yet his black hair neatly combed over his soon-to-be bald, fair, white skin showed the stress on his forty-year-old body. His lanky frame was exaggerated by a custom-tailored suit mismatched for his body—a business jacket that hung over his shoulders made him resemble a little boy dressed in his father's clothes.

I pulled my hand out from my portfolio, floundering on my high-heeled shoes, using the strength of my elbow to hold my brief bag back to keep it from smacking his hand as soon as I went in for a handshake. His doe eyes squinted at my palm as if trying to read a name inscribed on my skin. The phone on his desk rang, washing a look of uncertainty off his face. With my hand still stretched out, his hand grabbed the phone, but the tangled cord didn't offer enough length to reach his ear. Tilting his head to the side, he brought his face four inches off his desk to keep the cord from yanking itself out of the wall.

I stared at him in silence, waiting for his cue to speak.

"Your previous experience?" Hala said, bringing my gaze to meet her eyes.

"*Marhaba*," Dr. Mohammad yelled into the phone. My neck whipped back towards his attention.

"Your previous experience?" Hala pulled my gaze back to her attention to get a glance of her annoyance.

"Zain, zain, zain," Dr. Mohammad shouted over Hala.

"Your experience advising internationals?" She coughed.

"La, la, la," Dr. Mohammad blared.

I was as unfamiliar with Middle Eastern culture as I was with Arabic—nothing cued me in to determine how to read the room. I needed one of those translating headsets worn at the United Nations. Dr. Mohammad wrenched his neck to hold the landline between his ear and his shoulder, grasping my résumé in one hand while texting with the other. He narrowed his eyebrows while glancing at my résumé.

"Occidental? What's that?" he asked of my alma mater.

"Ya know Barack Obama?" I quipped. "He also went there."

Dr. Mohammad squinted trying to interpret my banter. I stared back, trying to translate his body language. Hala rolled her eyes, carrying on with the interview.

"*Hamdulillah*," Dr. Mohammad shouted, looking up at the ceiling. "*Mashallah*." His face lowered to the receiver. "*Shukran, Shukran, Shukran*," he repeated until the last moment when he hung up the phone, asking Hala, "We are done here, no?"

Hala ushered me out of the room through a backdoor labeled emergency only. *That's it?* I wondered, *After traveling three hours for a twenty-minute interview.* Leaving with more questions than they asked, I found myself sitting alone on the curb, waiting for my ride, wondering how I got here, praying the City of Angels would keep a nice Jewish girl safe.

Chapter 2

Temping For Peanuts

*T*wo weeks after the job interview marked my sixth month unemployed. A temp agency placement kept me afloat, offering a weekly paycheck with just a five-minute commute to Hillcrest, the gay mecca of San Diego. Pleasant Surprises was a business that packaged and shipped gourmet food bouquets. The brick and mortar storefront often confused men in the neighborhood who would excitedly pop in for a glance, hoping it was a massage parlor of sorts. The bell tied to the front door chimed, cueing the sleazebag who rented the office space across the hall for filming freelance porn to peep his head out to see who was coming.

"Look up. Align the box. Pull the cord. Fill the box. Move on to the next one. Got it?" Noah, the owner of the gift basket shop, instructed me. His unbuttoned collared shirt showed off the dark brown rug growing on his chest. Tilting my head back to look up, I could see him pointing to a fitted sheet hooked up to a hacked pulley system that with a tug of the cord, using just the right amount of tension, would release hundreds of packaging peanuts into the cardboard box I just finished taping together. "When you need more nuts, you'll go outside…." his voice trailed off as I followed behind him.

"Down there," Noah said, pointing to a door in the alley-way next to a locked garbage bin. "When the nuts run out," he repeated. Eight foot tall bags of Styrofoam peanuts took up space in a storage unit on the backside of the building, two flights down the metal stairs that reeked of trash and urine. My job was to tiptoe down the landing without startling any of the homeless men sleeping under the awning, unlock the door, throw the bag over my shoulder, and dart back up the stairs.

There were three of us on the job but only two of us sweating bullets. Noah had one full-time employee, Krishna, a young female from India, who followed every order as if it was a request. She expressed her gratitude for having the job by not saying a word as she worked around the clock, always compliant, never questioning or complaining.

"Let's just skip lunch." Noah's demand came out as a suggestion tied with a bow, as I stood staring through the cellophane at the food baskets I was wrapping. "Skip lunch," he repeated like a cuckoo bird that came out from behind the doors just to tweet the same sentence every day at noon and then retreat to its place, only reappearing to say, "Get through orders, cuckoo, get through orders, cuckoo." With the reces-sion dictating the terms of the job, there was no arguing with this cuckoo bird who only hires women and sends them to a back alley for peanuts.

"You Jewish?" Noah asked my fourth week of temping. Surrounded by presents wrapped in red and green ribbon, he added, "You look it."

I felt accosted by his blatancy, but I was Jewish; it wasn't like it was something I hid. I nodded my head and replied, "Yeah," pretending to be too distracted by the packaging process.

"Yeah, me too. Modern Orthodox," he said as if we shared something in common. "What kind of Jew are you?"

Duct-taping a box together, I say, "Reform" in a hushed voice as if I'm talking to the box and telling it to shape up.

"Oh, you're not *that* Jewish," he responded.

I peeked out of the corner of my eye to see if Krishna heard him. *I swear we are not all like that*, the voice in my head yelled, hoping Krishna could hear my thoughts. But no words came out of my mouth. The heat rising in my body, as if signaling a flight response, made it feel safer to be in the back alley. I placed a five-foot box directly in front of my face so I didn't have to look at him; it felt safer with a wall between us.

"Let's do a late night," Noah called out at 5 p.m. For seven dollars and fifty cents an hour, I considered giving him pushback, but worried that ruffling anything other than the cellophane gift wrap would result in Krishna getting a holiday card in the form of a pink slip. I felt like a Jewish elf tying bows for an Orthodox grinch, trying not to get accosted while going outside for peanuts. As a temp, averaging forty thousand spoken words a day, I stood for ten hours in the room with no one to talk to.

★ ★ ★

Pouring myself into my fiancé Tyrone's arms at home was my reward for surviving the day. He was a tall glass of chocolate milk, and I was parched. Tyrone was everything I wasn't—6'2" with his afro combed out, dressed in a collared button-down shirt and pressed khakis. It was evident that he'd spent most of his life in San Diego; his California vibe matched his outfit, relaxed and paired with flip-flops. Tyrone's brilliance shined with a nonchalance like the soccer mom van he cruised around in. He was confident in his practical ride with a very subtle coolness to it, the Thule rack on top for weekend excursions. During his college years in Colorado, he spent his free time snowboarding backcountry trails he and his friends would navigate wearing avalanche packs. Tyrone ran up the corporate biotech ladder, while my temp job afforded me the challenge of thinking twice before buying an iced mocha that cost an hour's worth of work.

Unlike Tyrone, I moved once a year every year since I was fifteen and was driving the car my dad bought me, which could fit all of my belongings. In my free time, I would run around my block with a fanny pack that carried my cell phone, two water bottles, a snack, and a couple of chill pills—just in case my heart started racing. We both grew up going to religious schools, our families engaged in their separate communities. My great-great-grandfather was the first rabbi of his temple; Tyrone's grandfather was a deacon at his Baptist church. I considered myself religious, but Tyrone would prove to have enough faith for both of us.

When the phone rang at nine o'clock that night, my head rested on a burnt orange bolster, my body sinking into the crook of a rickety brown suede futon. I squinted my eyes long enough to recognize the number as Dr. Mohammad's. Too tired to deal with anyone else, I let it go straight to voicemail, not feeling desperate enough to answer the call.

Playing the message the next morning, there was a bad connection, leaving me to piece the call together. My eyebrows narrowed as if trying to see a puzzle I was attempting to solve. I made out, "Academic advisor...salary...new office space."

I returned the phone call to hear Dr. Mohammad explain, "The Consulate of Kuwait...startup opportunity...advising on scholarships...counseling college students...landmark location. Are you willing to move to LA?" Dr. Mohammad asked, followed by, "Can you start Monday?"

Can I start Monday? I wondered. *I can't* ruminated all day, every day—the thoughts ran on a loop like a hamster on a wheel, exhausting my body while getting nowhere. But from where I stood, the idea of jumping into the rat race sounded like a step in the right direction. My anxiety made every decision for me, every step of the way. I knew better but wondered, *Could I start Monday?* Could I challenge myself and get away without it following?

"Yes?" I answered before I could stop myself, before I could get in my own way, before I talked myself out of it. I repeated, "Yes," without discussing it with the two people who knew me to say *I can't*: my therapist and fiancé.

Chapter 3

Till Death Do You Part

"Ŋ̤ou will get worse before you get better," the therapist said, unwavering, in our third one-hour session. It didn't take more than the few sessions over a six month period for her to note my mind was in a state of constant distress. She was a young woman who was studying to get her license in family and marriage therapy. While I wasn't married and didn't have a family, she needed to accrue her training hours, and I needed help that I could afford, working on gaining miles, being able to wander beyond a twenty-mile radius. I gauged that she was about my age, which made it feel like she was a friend who was in beauty school, and I was being spun around in the salon chair while she practiced using razor-sharp scissors that could cut without even closing the blades.

"Okay now, close your eyes and visualize yourself getting into the car..." Natasha said in a soothing voice. "Remember to breathe. In through your nose, out through your mouth.

Inhale, hold your breath, and then exhale, letting everything go." The intention of the breath work was to practice being calm, but this setting was anything but relaxing. "Think about your goal while you visualize yourself succeeding," she continued.

This is so stupid. Of course, I can see myself driving when I close my eyes—such a waste of time. I could be at yoga right now, actually relaxing instead of focusing on forcing myself to not be anxious. I'm so hungry. What am I going to make for dinner? I think I have chicken in the fridge. Mmmmmm, I should pick up some artichokes on the way home. What else do I need at the store?

"Picture yourself in the car, turning on the engine, and thinking about where you are driving to."

Butter. Butter, cream, and artichokes. Butter, cream, artichokes, and rice. Remember these four things at the store.

"Be present. Where are you turning now?"

Ughhhhhh, I can't remember my grocery list while giving directions. I give in to the exercise, readjusting my thoughts to get back on the road. "I'm making a right turn onto the freeway, heading north on the Five towards La Jolla," I say with my eyes closed.

"Notice the road signs passing overhead as you drive underneath them. Look at the cars ahead of you. Feel the comfort of your seat as your hands continue to grasp the steering wheel." Not knowing which way to go, the therapist advised, "Don't return to where you started." Challenging me to push through without looking back, she added, "When you are uncomfortable, pause, regroup, and then move forward. What do you see ahead of you?"

My stomach churned, and my white knuckles fought to crank the steering wheel. It was stuck, and so was I. I just wanted to retreat, to turn back to where it was safe, to that point in my life where the pain wasn't as intense, where it didn't decide which roads I could take. Now I couldn't even dream of adventure without suffering. That was taken away too. My fear sat in the driver's seat, and I was dragged along.

The visualization had taken me back to my fifteen-year-old self, on a 107-degree summer day in New Mexico, sitting idly in the back seat while my parents drove us to a diner to meet their friend Judy for lunch. They had jumped out of the car ahead of me and walked hurriedly into the restaurant, more eager to order than they were to wait for me. An alarm sounded when I pushed down on the handle of the car door, trying to get out. My parents neglected to notice I wasn't right behind them or that when they pressed the key fob, it immediately locked me in. I was a teenager fighting a child safety feature that sounded the car alarm when I tried to get out from the inside once the fob engaged the locks from the outside. I banged on the tinted window in desperation, begging for someone to hear me screaming over the car alarm that startled no one. A dead cell phone left in the car, with no service in the desert anyway, only taunted me by hanging from the cord of the charger as a reminder that I too lacked power. I tried to get the attention of a stranger who didn't know how to help. "I think she's stuck in there," I could hear the faint voice of a couple pointing at me as I nodded my head, like a caged animal at the zoo.

My mother waited in line to place an order, while my father eventually came outside of the air-conditioned restaurant to see what was taking me so long. As he walked towards the car, the anticipation was instantly quelched by the look of fury on his face.

"God damn it, Jessica," he said, slamming the car door behind me. I leaped out, keeping my mouth shut.

While guilt and anger aren't genetic, anxiety disguises itself in many ways. The loss of control for him translated into anger that concerned strangers were pointing fingers, causing a scene he wanted nothing to do with, as I struggled, restrained by the heat of my thoughts burning throughout my body. But when I got out of the car, there was no relief. The fire extinguished, but the burns scarred.

I kept my head down, walking to our table, where my mother sat texting on her phone, only looking up when she heard my father shouting, "Goddamn it." The explosive yelling was predictable, even inside the restaurant, but the volatile blame now made the car seem safer.

My mother looked at me to put together what was happening and then looked back at my father as he threatened to go, "I don't need this bullshit."

"Oh Stan, don't go," she said, more concerned with how we appeared to others than how we would get home without him. "We all want you to be here."

My mother looked at me, cueing me to apologize. "I'm sorry," I said, required to look my father in his eyes. "It was my fault." My voice trembled as my body was writhing in pain. "I'm fine." He shoved his chair back away from the table, arms crossed.

"I'm not eating."

My mother mouthed to me, "Do not disappoint your father," as their friend Judy walked towards us.

Masking the pain was the only apology that would be accepted. Acting as if my body wasn't trembling with fear was the only way to make it go away, at least temporarily. I knew sitting there in silence was not an option. I would now have to put on a show.

I lowered my pitch as I spoke to keep the words leaving my mouth from quivering, to participate in a conversation that I could barely hear over my thoughts, at the busy restaurant where my opinion was as irrelevant as my voice.

The moment Judy arrived at the table, I grinned for everyone to see. "Right behind you," the waiter said, swiveling around with his tray, filled to the brim. It weighed on his arms like the silence that dangled over our table, about to be broken.

"Just in time," Judy said, scooting into the booth next to me, trapping me in the corner across from my father.

I gagged at the smell of the food placed in front of us. "Mmmmm," I said, trying to keep myself from throwing up at the table. Showing my remorse meant choking down the plate of poached eggs served over black beans and potatoes smothered in cheese and green chiles as if nothing happened.

"Can I get you anything else?" I could faintly hear the waiter ask in the background while I kept my eyes from flooding with tears.

"What are you thinking?" Natasha asks me, interrupting the memory and bringing me back to the therapy session. I'm sitting in silence with my eyes still closed as I feel a teardrop down my face. Another one follows it. I keep my eyes shut tight, but the tears somehow continue to escape.

"What do you see?" Natasha asked.

My eyes opened, feeling hypnotized into defeat. "I can't go any further." I shook. The heat spread through my body like a volcano just waiting to erupt. My mind spewing flames, burning deeper and deeper through the scars. I needed help, and I needed it now.

"Your time is up," she said, turning her back to me.

★ ★ ★

For the twelve mile drive home from the therapist's office, I saw red—the brake lights in front of me, a punch to my gut, tormented my thoughts. As the cars inched down the freeway, I gagged on a metallic taste as if I was licking the steel that surrounded my body, anxiety weighing heavily on my chest. With the windows down and the air conditioning working to cool my thoughts, I gasped for air, unable to catch my breath. The tighter I clenched the steering wheel, the less of a grip I had, my hands dripping with sweat. My mind sat in the driver's seat while my body tagged along for the ride.

In tunnel vision, I tried to focus on the road. Surveying the surrounding drivers, I wondered, *Who would help me when I couldn't help myself?* Without blood hemorrhaging my body, no one could see me dying a death by my own thoughts.

I can hear the therapist saying, "The only way to move forward is to go through it. The walls cave in when you stay still." But my thoughts were louder.

I can't manage…not without Tyrone. What if he died…and I hadn't? I'd be alone…waiting to die. Wouldn't last a single day… I don't even think… Could I manage being in the coffin by myself? We'll have to share a coffin…. I'll lay there dead…waiting for him to die. That's it…my only option. I'll have to die first.

The illogical thoughts screamed in my head while I suffered in silence. I wore the panic like a backpack, shouldering the weight as it came along everywhere I tried to go and anywhere I wanted to be. Interpreting the anxiety as shame, the panic a boulder to bear, the two merged into a roadblock between me and the life I wanted to live. Tyrone was a dream, but at thirty-one years old, my thoughts flooded with nightmares of "what-if's." Doubting my ability constantly, I wondered if like my anxiety, *I* was a burden.

Back at home, I laid one side of my head directly on an ice pack to soothe my face from the grinding of my jaw, unsure of how I made it back without melting into a puddle on the side of the road. My outsides looked nothing like my insides—the pain felt like an infection running through my blood, going through my mind, cueing my thoughts to hemorrhage, causing the space around me to yet again start to crumble as the radius of my comfort zone diminished. Dental insurance, or any form of health insurance for that matter, was too far out of reach.

Scrolling through photos on my flip phone, playing tricks on my mind to distract it, was the only tool I had while I waited for a sedative to kick in. A pixelated photo pieced itself together like a puzzle, yet before it all came into view, I could already see the image. Tyrone and I were grinning ear to ear, wearing t-shirts in a storm, our bodies held up by the old rusted bikes we owned years ago when we had storage. We had lugged them onto the train to ride along the clear paths in Santa Barbara. Ill-prepared for the weather but unphased by it, we paused to capture the beauty of the landscape, blurred in the background of the photo. Unbothered by the rain, or any of the elements, the wind slapped our faces red, our hands linked together, squeezing tightly, weathering the storm together.

There were plenty of images in my mind of our adventures, visions that appeared, even with my eyes closed, while other memories were swept away by the fog of the sedatives that tagged along. I knew where I didn't want to be—without health insurance, a preexisting condition, no stable income, and maxed out on the number of times I could defer my student loans.

★ ★ ★

"You need a job, and this is the job you need," Tyrone had said matter-of-factly when no one else understood why I would take the job in LA. "It'll get you to where you want to be."

Tyrone knew me well enough to know LA would be a struggle every step of the way, likely ending in failure before it even got started. Yet he saw that my spirit wanted to fly, that my heart and desire to try hadn't been squelched by the realities in my head and the baggage I carried that had still been far too heavy to manage on my own.

In 2008, Tyrone and I had found ourselves unemployed amidst an economic crisis. With the country starving for work, we were hungry for job opportunities, realizing this wasn't the time for menu planning and cake tastings. The economy was too unstable to be reckless. Tyrone secured a decent job six months prior, allowing us to move from a one-bedroom month to month rental to signing a year lease on a two bedroom mid-century craftsman house in a walk-able family neighborhood, where he saw our future.

I hadn't even started the job and I was already wondering how long I would have to stay in it, going back and forth in my mind, trying to calculate how long it would take for this job to lead me to an opportunity in San Diego, to bring me back to the life I worked so hard to live. "This is the job you need," Tyrone reassured me. While I wondered how long I would last in LA, he added, "You know I can't go this time, right?"

Tyrone studied every book around him, planning his future that shined as bright as his clear path ahead. Like everything he observed, he knew how to read my silence.

"This is the job you need," he reassured me.

I tried to focus on his steady voice soothing my soul, but my internal thoughts kept interrupting. Was this my last chance to see if I could survive on my own? Nine years together—and only seven months from our wedding—I doubted how Tyrone felt, if he was okay with me leaving, if he wondered what it meant for our relationship, what it meant for our future.

"Come on, I'll help you pack." His voice cooed, "Added bonus, your parents are in town that weekend. They can drive you up."

Chapter 4

Entering The Fortress

1 booked a hotel room for two nights, four blocks away from my new job, where I woke up alone. I could feel the cold air-conditioning coming from the wall unit as I lay sweating. My aching limbs were keeping me from getting up. A warm shower would help, but throwing cold water on my face would more likely awaken me from my drowsy state. Another dose of cold medicine was not going to mix well with coffee. I would have to pick one or the other. I would be too shaky and feel more on edge if I combined the two. This was not the way I wanted to start the first day on the job. Despite having prepared the night before, laying everything out, executing my plan now seemed ambitious.

I felt a shortness of breath as soon as I zipped up my dress. I assured myself that it was only a cold and rationalized the restrictive feeling was due to how the piece was tailored to be tight in the chest. Scanning the room, looking for my keys, I was startled by my reflection. I saw white. With a cold clouding my mind, I now doubted my judgment. Every part of me looked like it was showing off my skin. The dress I bought from Banana Republic was conservative and stylish. When I tried it on in the store, it looked fitting for the new job, in the dimly lit dressing room with the slanted mirrors that have a slimming effect. Now, I no longer noticed the dress. The bright fluorescent light shining down on me highlighted my white skin.

I thought back to the interview, picturing Hala with her head unveiled, but every other part of her was covered. I searched through my suitcase to find a pair of cropped black pressed trousers. I reached my arm through the leg to find the stockings left tucked into a ball from the last time I wore them. I kicked off my shoes and pulled the pair of black, lace tights up my legs, praying they wouldn't snag them in my haste. Glancing back at the mirror, I didn't notice the delicate pattern of circles swirling tightly around my legs; all I noticed were my white arms staring back at me. Arriving on time seemed more important than the short-sleeved dress that now felt like the wrong choice. I reached my arm to the bottom of the front pocket of the suitcase, where my underwear was shoved, feeling around for a soft laced cotton garment with strings attached. I stretched my arm out to pull a black scarf from the bottom. I whirled it around my shoulders as if wrapping myself into a tornado. The new dress no longer shined with luster in the mirror, but my skin was now covered to step out in LA—in eighty-degree weather. Short on time, I headed to the new job, hiding under all of the layers.

★ ★ ★

"First time?" A man in a dark suit, tinted glasses, and an earpiece asked, standing inches away from my body as I stared up at the Century City twin towers, mouth propped open, counting the number of stories. Arms crossed, he stood blocking the heavy glass doors behind him. "Forty-four," he said, reading my lips. I thought the eighteenth was bad. "Guests over there," he said, tilting his head to point out a security detail behind a front desk. An indistinguishable security guard manned every entrance, all dressed in the same suit, surrounding the building, verifying everyone's identity before allowing access. The tower was a fortress.

The lobby entrance of the building with a triangular footprint looked like the inside kaleidoscope. Shimmering lights sparkled through the floor to ceiling glass windows that were three stories high. With the elevators tucked away, the mesmerizing twinkle of the color shined through, distracting an audience of the jobs that took place behind closed doors.

"Who ya visiting?" the next security guard asked, standing in front of a shiny slab of marble.

"It's my first day," I said with a grin.

"Driver's license," he said, scanning my ID and all 5'2" of me. "Ya gonna need clearance. Forty-third floor," he said, handing me a temporary security pass.

"You mean the eighteenth?"

"Security clearance first. Forty-third floor. This way," he said, leading me to the elevator after cueing my mind to start playing a round of "death-by-elevator." *Forty-third… Forty-third… Forty-third…* echoed through my head. At the front of the line to enter the elevator, I didn't know how I was still standing on my own two feet. The metal doors opened, sucking businessmen into it like a magnet, pulling their bodies forward, trapping them inside the walls. I was incapable of turning around. With the pressure of the swarming people flooding the space, I would have to push through the crowd to escape, causing a scene that would bring too much-unwanted attention from the security guards. I exhaled, letting all the used air out of my lungs before taking in the largest inhale possible, believing it could be my last. I held onto that one breath.

The distressed voice in my head announced a warning with a shrill that pierced my soul as the instrumental music played over the intercom. "Ladies and gentlemen, welcome to your turn to play Russian roulette. Please step inside as death awaits you." That last step forward meant I was choosing to play. I was now in the death trap.

There was no fresh air to breathe. *You are going to pee your pants and then die. You will be completely silent as you embarrass yourself suffocating. Your body will collapse, but you won't be able to fall down—there won't be enough space. You will have died in an upright position. Look at the people around you—these are the people that you are going to die in front of. They are in their fancy clothes, and they will be looking at you bewildered. There will be nothing they can do to save you. They will try to call for help, make a measly attempt, and then start worrying about themselves. You won't be able to breathe until someone from the outside arrives. But no one will be able to come for hours—by then, it will be too late. There is no way out now. There is no way to escape.*

When my vision started to blur, I wondered how I was in this place. The outlandish thoughts and the outrageous game were unavoidable. My mind was rolling the dice, and my body was just trying to deal with the cards already dealt. There was no sense to make of it. I couldn't talk myself out of it or explain it to others. I knew the game inside and out, especially where fear liked to play, and yet every time, I got caught off guard.

On the forty-third floor, a flash went off, capturing a photo of my body drenched in sweat. A blank white electronic pass associated with my identity gave clearance to access the eighteenth floor, the lobby, and the basement. The electronic record identified each person, time-stamping your entrance into the building, the elevator, and the office suite. Riding back down, I tried to catch my breath, clutching the security pass with my white knuckles, believing its only job was to help identify bodies easier.

On the eighteenth floor, the elevator opened long enough to spit me out to find floor-to-ceiling doors, with the electronic security system discreetly camouflaged into the stark white walls that gave a dramatic entryway to the educational division of the Consulate of Kuwait. Yet one door was propped open by a three-ring binder, allowing me to walk through into the busy office without using the identity badge, where no one on the inside noticed I arrived.

★ ★ ★

From my seat in Dr. Mohammad's office, I could see for miles. We were so high up; it felt like the sun was renting space nearby, showing off its brilliance as its rays bounced off the buildings. The cars were so far below; they'd resemble shooting stars if rush hour wasn't every minute of the day, prohibiting them, and everyone else, from moving forward in life.

Meanwhile, Dr. Mohammad's office was a human traffic jam. Advisors flooded through the door, waving their arms around with student files, shouting, "It's urgent," each one louder than the next. Dr. Mohammad was on his cell phone when a call came in on his landline. He was scribbling down notes on the corner of any piece of paper he could find amongst the clutter of official government documents that covered his desk. Dr. Mohammad listened to a call on a landline, holding his hand over the mouthpiece, while speaking into his US cell phone, held by his shoulder meeting his ear. Hala ran into the room holding another cell, his Kuwaiti line, up in the air, twirling it like a baton, to get his attention. Draping the landline over his shoulder, Dr. Mohammad waved his arm frantically for Hala, hurrying her over. "Come," he mouthed to her, to jot down what the frantic parent was saying, trading the US cell phone for the Kuwaiti flip phone.

In the brief moment that Dr. Mohammad wasn't on the phone, advisors continued to flood his office, handing him papers and pointing to where he needed to sign off. As the only advisor seated, I was invisible, trying to be transparent with my words. "Still need to sign the contract. What we discussed over the phone."

Dr. Mohammad sat at an exaggeratedly long, custom ordered mahogany executive's desk, in a dark leather chair, facing my direction, with his gaze on the door behind me, his back turned, blocking him from seeing the floor to ceiling windows that showed a 180-degree view of the city of stars. "Inshallah, your salary will be approved," he said, his words breaking my gaze to bring my attention back to the flurry of advisors racing inside his office and around his desk, vying for his attention. My eyes narrowed, unsure of his words. "Until the ministry approves, I will have to pay you out of my own pocket," he said, momentarily glancing towards me to gauge my reaction.

I could hear Tyrone's voice in my head asking, "What do you mean they don't have clearance to pay you?"

"Inshallah," Dr. Mohammad repeated, looking up at the ceiling. "May it be as God wills it."

While the US was in a financial drought, the Gulf flooded in its petroleum-based economy. Our prestigious suite, in a notable zip code, rented at $400,000 a month, and I worked without a desk. Dr. Mohammad was the director of our office, and he rented a house for $36,000 a month, paid for by the Kuwaiti government. They covered the luxury vehicles shipped from Kuwait and the chauffeur that drove Dr. Mohammad to and from his home, which was a mile away in Beverly Hills, and yet I lacked a contract detailing a salary. There was a budget for a tea boy, someone who brings tea around to serve, but no office supplies. Dr. Mohammad's pockets seemed to be so deep that for now, I was more concerned with taking the elevator.

Ultimately, my lack of response didn't matter to Dr. Mohammad. There hadn't been a moment to say anything. His attention was already back to signing off on the papers shoved in front of him. Directed into the conference room, the space would work as my office until the ministry approved the purchase of additional office furniture.

My heightened senses were already working overtime when I felt someone's eyes scanning me up and down: "You look like a teacher in a winter storm," I heard a woman say with a biting laugh. I was covered in what a Jewish mother would want her daughter to wear to High Holy Day services. LA was a fashion capital, but this was not the place to take risks. Without introducing herself, the advisor dropped fifty files on the table. Nahla was the third advisor hired, which she deemed as authority to be rude. Mexican and Muslim, she stood with her nose up, above the others, at six feet tall in her stiletto heels. She smiled at me, leaving the room. *Maybe I read her wrong.* But then she came back. Without saying a word, she abandoned an even bigger load, dropping them onto the floor. I lugged the massive stack of files up onto the table. The weight of the stacks grew heavier, yet her caseload lightened. Three hundred student files looked like confetti thrown around the conference room. "Good luck," she sneered.

From my seat, the outside world seemed far away. Peering out the window from this high, the people looked like ants moving around, following clearly outlined paths. Meanwhile, I opened the first file, unsure of where to start, leaning back into the wobbling swivel chair that now added to the unbalanced chaos that whirled around my body.

Order was a necessity. Step one: alphabetize. Starting with the As, I looked through all three hundred files. "A" was the first letter of 279 of the last names. Alabdullah, Al Abdullah, Albdulah. *Are all of these students related? How do they tell each other apart? How do I tell them apart?* First names spelled out with as much clarity as the last: "Mohammad, Mohamed, Mohamad, Mohaned, Muhanad." Reviewing passports and high school transcripts didn't offer clarity. The name of a student spelled three different ways on three separate documents seemed to be normal.

After two hours of reading through the files, I longed for some direction. I tapped on the open door to Dr. Mohammad's right-hand woman, Ashley, a twenty-five-year-old, busty, American brunette who signed PhD after her name.

"Hey, d'ya have a sec?" I asked in an enthusiastic voice.

"Nope," she replied with a grin that left me hanging. She smiled, using her chin to point out the seat in front of her. "But go ahead." Her hands and gaze continued to type away without missing a beat.

She was Dr. Mohammad's confidant and ear for listening; her boyfriend's uncle was Dr. Mohammad's college roommate and "American brother." Unequivocally, this made her the favorite child, addressing Dr. Mohammad using words like a lollipop, both serving to pacify and gratify his constant demands. He trusted very few people. However, based on her indirect bloodline to his best friend, Ashley was his chosen one. I knew she played an important role as soon as I took stock of her office. Her furniture mirrored Dr. Mohammad's with a smaller version of his mahogany executive desk and dark leather chair. But unlike Dr. Mohammad's desk, covered in official government documents spread out on top of stacks of files and invoices with six figure numbers circled in red ink and a calculator, Ashley's desk had a computer and a Montblanc pen next to monogrammed Post-it notes. But it was the copier/printer in the corner that captured my eye. It stood out like a ham sandwich in the office's halal kitchen. Everyone else was left to fight over the one in the hall.

"Is there like an HR?" I asked.

Ashley laughed, shaking her head. "Don't need it. Don't abide by American labor laws anyway."

"Any advice ?"

"Respond to the students immediately, or a parent will call," she explained. "Have every email printed out for evidence. When Dr. Mohammad yells for you, you better have 'em all there." I wondered why she made our jobs sound like we were under investigation. Ashley typed away at her computer, adding, "Basically, get ready to put out fires."

From her open office door, I could hear the staff continuing to run up and down the hallway to fight over the only printer that was next to an old fax machine that sent out the endless requests, the only manner of communication with the Ministry of Higher Education, which seldom spit out a reply. The fast-paced office competed to get their documents printed first and run to Dr. Mohammad's office for signature, running back to make a copy, fax the document and then copy the fax receipt. It was required to print out every email, from each student, along with our response, hole punch, and then clip it into the student file. A country with a landscape of desert, filled with oil, didn't notice the number of trees missing.

There was no server or database, just Excel sheets and individually created Gmail accounts. Similar to the staff's interactions with each other—nothing was connecting us. We spent the bulk of our time waiting in line for Dr. Mohammad to approve our letters of student requests. We were asking permission from Dr. Mohammad to ask for permission from the ministry.

"If I have any questions…?" I started.

"Don't ask me." She shrugged. "Call DC," she said, referring to our counterparts at the other office.

Our office was the cultural division of the Consulate of Kuwait, established on the west coast to focus on the students studying in surrounding regions. Due to the rising number of scholarships issued by the Ministry of Higher Education of Kuwait, we were an extension of the Cultural Office of the Embassy located in Washington, DC.

The Kuwaiti government offered full scholarships to promote cross-cultural understanding through university studies in the US and a diverse list of countries worldwide. Any Kuwaiti national seeking this opportunity abroad must meet the minimum qualifications to receive the ultimate reward, a full scholarship to college along with all the amenities covered. As the number of students on scholarships grew exponentially over the years, perspective became blurred, privilege seemed like entitlement to others.

The LA division established itself to take on the western half of DC's caseloads. Nearly ten thousand Kuwaiti students enrolled at US institutions of higher education. The DC office employed seventy-nine staffers to manage the caseloads for this scholarship program, which was established in their office in the 1950s. Our office of twelve loosely came together by the spring of 2009 and felt like a startup, with high stakes of reputations on the line. The majority of our caseloads lay in strewn boxes across the floor labeled in Arabic for Nubia, the translator, to sort through when she wasn't busy gossiping with Hala.

Ashley handed me a document from the top of her desk. "You're welcome," she grinned, showing me a cheat sheet of general information. The paper was a photocopy of a fax in Arabic, originally sent to the DC office from Kuwait in the '80s. Forwarded to our office, again via fax, it came through with barely any ink left in the machine. A pink streak marked the document, from top to bottom, smudging the letters. Pulling the paper closer into view, a faint pencil from years prior earmarked the corner with notes in English. With her fingers pressing the document on her desk, "You'll have to make your own copy," she noted, "down the hall."

★ ★ ★

At lunchtime, I heard the shuffling of feet followed by absolute silence. I walked down the hall, pretending to look for office supplies, the ones I already knew didn't exist, to find the entire suite empty. When the clock struck twelve, I turned back into my fifteen-year-old self. I had sat in the backseat of the car for the two weeks my parents spent driving across the country as we moved from Washington, DC, to New Mexico. I didn't know that being the new girl in a small town would challenge who I thought I was. I had grown up with all the kids in my neighborhood and was confident in my bearings. I wanted to be home, where I belonged, but I knew better than to say anything as my parents bickered about the move the entire drive while I sat inches away, pretending not to be there.

Day one of the new job took me back to my fifteen-year-old self on the first day of high school in New Mexico, where I knew no one, not a single friend within two thousand miles. Being out on the grass in the courtyard would have been way too obvious—everyone would see that I was sitting alone at lunch. I grabbed my gym bag to be conspicuous and headed away from the groups of friends gathering so inherently it resembled a school of fish. I went to the one place I could think of, where no one else would be, and sat down on a wooden bench in the last row of the girls' locker room, where I could hear if someone opened the door, allowing me enough time to shove my lunch back in my bag, rattle a locker, and pretend as if I was getting ready. I pulled out the brown paper bag and sat in silence, hoping no one would open the door to see that I was alone.

By day three in the office, Liz asked me to lunch. She and I were two of the three Americans working there. As Dr. Mohammad's right hand, Ashley was off-limits to have a real conversation, but Liz and I didn't have to edit ourselves the way we would with the others.

"You're advisor number eight," Liz let me know. She started the job a few days before, making her lucky number seven, catching me up on all the pieces she put together, by herself, when no one else would talk to her.

"Whatever you do, don't shut your door."

"What do you mean?"

"The doctor has a thing about the doors being shut," Dr. Mohammad had warned Liz. "The words must be the same in front and behind."

Finding a table outside in the courtyard, I rolled my lunch out into sections. Liz preferred snacks at her desk, leaving my lunch taking over the table. Unfolding a pouch of aluminum foil, I nibbled on my bacon-wrapped dates.

"Ya got a lot of chutzpah eating those." She winked, not needing her degree from Yale to recognize that I was Jewish.

I grinned in response, feeling at ease. I recognized her east coast energy but also sensed that she was trying to break free of that mold. I loved to cook; she loved to bake. I found searing the liver of a chicken more forgiving than the precision and focus needed to make her chocolate chip shortbread, which required enough patience to sift the flour three times. I graduated from a college no one heard of and was desperate to establish my career in international education in San Diego. Liz graduated from Yale and, after a stint in movie production, decided to try something new.

"How'd ya end up in California?" I asked.

"I wanted some space from the East Coast," she replied.

"The whole coast?" I laughed.

"Long story short, my parents dropped my brother off at medical school. The same university my father studied at. No one spoke the whole ride home."

"Oh," I said, shaking my head, not understanding.

"My brother yelled 'Fuck off' to my family, and my dad shouted, 'No, you fuck off,' and before campus safety arrived, I was stuck in the backseat of the car ride home."

"I got you," I said. From then on, we ate lunch together every day.

Chapter 5

Ring Off The Hook

"*P*ut your money under the sun and reap in the shade," Dr. Mohammad said, day four, handing me the formal paperwork with the heading, "Salaries and Benefits." I scanned the two-page document detailing the "Monthly Emoluments." Airplane tickets, conferences, and the maximum amount of bonus money, in Kuwaiti dinar, allocated for good work. The Kuwaiti government offered money for almost everything under the sun.

Unfortunately for the staff, this list was for the students on scholarships we advised. A column with the heading "Entitlements" listed university tuition, monthly salary, and book and clothing allowance twice a year. Students could receive cash bonuses for grade point averages above 3.2, as well as up to three round trip tickets to Kuwait, or the equivalent in cash, over four years of university studies.

Advisors sent the accountants lists of students receiving "allowance." Issued on the twenty-third of every month, these payments allowed the students to pay rent before the first of the following month. Meanwhile, I had no idea when I was getting my first paycheck. I headed down the hallway to the back corner where the two accountants doing the job of thirty could be found working fifteen hour days. Viraj was Canadian, Christian, single, and in his early forties. He had worked at an embassy in DC for over a decade but paced himself so Abdul Baatin, his kindhearted, 115-pound, Muslim, Sudanese supervisor, wouldn't fall apart. They were setting up payroll for each student, wiring money from the Kuwaiti government directly to the students' US bank accounts. Viraj sat at his desk using his computer to double check Abdul Baatin's work performed in the adjacent office, using a calculator, a sheet of paper, and a ruler to follow the lines on the spreadsheet, saying each number out loud before typing it in, using only one finger.

"Any chance you know when the staff salaries are issued?" I asked Viraj.

He sighed with relief at the interruption, to see a human instead of a number. "I'm sorry," he said, shaking his head, offering a bowl with three hard candies in it. He pushed his chair away from the desk, turning his back to me and enjoying the opportunity to stretch, and reached on top of his file cabinet for an unopened bag of Swiss chocolates. "It's the only way I can tempt anyone to come say hi."

Turning back around, I noticed a slight tear in his pants, a bit of his dark skin showing through. His tie was loose around his neck, easing the chokehold that the office had on him. With the bowl refilled to the brim, he stretched out his arm, offering the rich dark chocolates. "This is all I have."

★ ★ ★

"Where's your diamond?" my coworker, Fatema asked, reaching over my arm to grab a coffee mug in the office kitchen. Her long, black hair shined like her outfit as she moved without a scarf on her head. A younger generation Muslim, she referred to her status as "single and stunning." Growing up in LA, she kept up with the latest fashions, distracting an audience from noticing she was fully covered. "Heard you're getting married. Where's your diamond?"

"It's not my thing." I grinned politely.

She squinted her eyes to see if she heard me right. "Weird." Her hands wrapped around the mug filled with steaming hot water, she shrugged and left the room, uninterested in an explanation.

A few years earlier, in the spring of 2007, I felt immobile laying on the ground of my apartment back in San Diego, dragging myself across the cold tile floor, hoping that the nausea had been from food poisoning from the late night taco truck we hit up the previous evening and not my anxiety. Tyrone was wearing a white collared shirt with the sleeves neatly rolled up. I could smell the Old Spice he put on after taking a hot shower while I looked pathetic in the same yoga pants I'd slept in the night before and worn to a few yoga classes without having washed them in between. With one leg crossed, Tyrone was sitting back reading a sports magazine on my futon, not alarmed at all by the sight of me laying on the floor in a fetal position. He reached into the pocket of his ironed khaki pants, pulled something out, and tossed a tiny, ring-sized box towards me. My sluggish reflexes jerked my sore body up to catch it, but it just ricocheted off my knee. *Now? Right now? He can't be serious.*

I couldn't see myself walking down an aisle with enough strength in my legs and my mind to get me to the end. I blamed my anxiety for keeping me from having Tyrone propose for seven years of our relationship. I said "I can't" in life so many times; I never thought I'd walk down an aisle to say "I do."

"Do not propose," I insisted to Tyrone for years while knowing one life together wouldn't be enough to hold all of the love I had for him.

"Pace yourself, Jess" was all Tyrone replied, unfazed by my demand. A tiny box sat upright while I laid like a puddle on the floor, unable to move my body. I waved my hand around as if reaching for a crystal ball to see what the future would hold.

Inside the box was a silver ring inscribed, "What barrier is there that love cannot break," a quote by Mahatma Gandhi.

"It's just a ring," Tyrone said, looking up from his magazine. "It's just to say when you reach a time that you're ready for me to propose, just let me know, cause I'm ready."

★ ★ ★

I had only stepped away from my phone for six minutes to reheat my coffee. When I had returned to my desk, the red light on my phone flashed, signaling my stomach to churn.

"You have twenty-seven new messages," my voice mail system alerted me. *This is bad*, I thought as the sinking feeling flooded my body. I played the messages one by one, hearing nothing but a phone hanging up. This is bad.

The second I finished playing all of the missed calls and put the phone back on the receiver, it immediately rang.

"I need my salary now," a student said sharply without greeting me on the phone or telling me his name. "Do you know how many times I've called?" he asked.

Twenty-seven?

"Why haven't you responded?" he replied, unfamiliar with the American practice of leaving your information at the sound of the tone.

"Salaries are issued the last week of the month," I reminded him, sugarcoating my tone. "All student salaries are issued the twenty-third of every month," I explained, unlike the twelve staff salaries that were issued whenever Abdul Baatin had time.

A message popped up on my screen, an IM from Liz. "No way Taco Bell's halal, right?" I google "halal" while listening to the student rant. "Don't think it's kosher," I IM'ed her back.

"I have no money to pay rent. Wha'da'u expect me to do?" he insisted, almost prodding me to answer.

"I completely understand," I said, unremorseful. I was working in the high-rent district, living out of my suitcase. My accommodations for a couple of weeks were a sleeping bag on the floor of a room in a shared apartment an old friend from New Mexico rented for $1,800 a month. Every morning, I rolled up my sleeping bag and tiptoed outside, to walk in pajamas, to my car parked on a busy road. I picked an outfit from my suitcase and swapped a sleeping bag for toiletries before heading back into the apartment to wait in line for the shower. All of my belongings were packed in the trunk, in a two-hour zone, which wouldn't get ticketed between 6 p.m. through 8 a.m. as long as it wasn't a street sweeping day. Aside from my life with Tyrone, everything I needed was in my car, the place that drove me to the edge.

"I want to introduce you to Mrs. Winston," Liz said, picking me up at my desk promptly at noon. "Don't bring your lunch," she advised. I wasn't familiar with the dietary restrictions of the office, but I trusted her judgment. "Who's Mrs. Winston?" I asked, tucking my shirt in to appear more polished.

"We're meeting her at a juice bar," Liz laughed with a wink.

Just outside of our office, I was still lost in translation. On our walk out, she taught me what she learned from a student's receipts: that a "juice bar" is considered kosher for some of the males who found themselves at strip clubs that didn't serve alcohol. I also learned that Mrs. Winston's was an actual salad and juice bar with locally sourced organic produce that resembled a rainbow of fresh colors ending with a pot of golden quinoa. Deep trays filled with pomegranate seeds waited next to avocado mash. The line started with a choice of arugula, kale, butter lettuce, or red cabbage and ended with sundried tomatoes, mandarin oranges, chilled jicama, whole grain orzo, kalamata olives, green onions, brown rice, and dried cranberries. Bell peppers rang a sweet tune from on top of my make-your-own gourmet salad to go. "This is my kind of cooking," Liz said. With unfamiliar options like sorghum, farro, persimmons, and fennel, I had a lot to learn.

As we walked back toward the office, she told me about the student with the Taco Bell receipts. Through Nubia's translations, she was able to decipher that he needed help budgeting. In reviewing his bank statements, Liz determined the student, here for a year of English language study, only spoke enough English to say "quesadilla" at the drive through window of a Taco Bell every day for a month.

★ ★ ★

"More?" Viraj asked on my eighth trip down the hall for chocolates that day.

"Keep 'em coming," I said as he opened a new bag.

"I think you need the good stuff," he said, reaching above his file cabinet, where I knew he hid the Swiss chocolates.

"You sure?" I asked, knowing I'd single-handedly consumed the majority of his stash.

"I'm still all on my own down here," he said. "I'm here more than I'm at home. I haven't even bought a bed yet."

"What?"

"I haven't unpacked my car from my move," he said.

I couldn't help but laugh. We were in the same boat. Bringing him into the fold, I asked, "Are *you* worried about someone breaking into your car?"

"Most of my stuff is busted up anyway," he said.

"Cheers to that?" I said, pretending to raise a glass with my chocolate in hand.

"Cheers to that," he said, both of us laughing away our sorrows as we unwrapped our chocolates.

Chapter 6

She Works Hard For Her Dinar

"Your first paycheck...." Dr. Mohammad trailed off, distracted by the text messages coming in through his phone. "You can't have it just yet." He said casually while I was in my sixth week on the job. I was five months from my wedding, and spent the money my parents gave me for a wedding dress to put down a deposit and pay the first month's rent. "Abdul Baatin must photocopy all of them with my signature and then fax the copy to the ministry."

"Thank you?" I replied.

I headed to the photocopy machine to uncover what the ministry approved for my salary. Twelve checks for the twelve employees laid face up, for all to see, on the table next to the photocopying machine, with no one in the hallway. Pretending to sort through my documents for copying, I scanned the table looking for my payday, unable to avoid checking to see what everyone else was making. Dr. Mohammad's signature on every check showed me everything I needed to see.

I hurried out of the office to call Tyrone. "What are you up to?"

"Working," he replied.

"They have my first paycheck. You won't believe it."

"They're paying you?" he said, unphased.

"They're paying me more than anyone else."

"Why do you know that?"

"Cause we don't follow American labor laws..." There was a silence over the line. "And Abdul Baatin left the paychecks out by the copier while he went outside to smoke. Do you think it was a mistake?" I asked Tyrone.

"That you looked at all the paychecks? Yep."

"No—the amount. You think it's a mistake?"

"Yep. You're worth way more." I could picture his grin. It always grounded me, offering me a true breath of fresh air.

Stepping back into the office, I found my paycheck in my coworker Dina's perfectly manicured hand. A shiny diamond sparkled on her ring finger. "All yours." She handed me the check with a memo attached, smiling as bright as the shimmering lip gloss she was wearing. Dina was stunning, kind, and as the third employee hired, one of Dr. Mohammad's favorites. "I'll help you get off the ground," she offered *him* at the job interview. Her newlywed glow went well with her dark silky brown hair, which swayed from side to side as she walked. She was Egyptian, born and raised in LA, and knew conversational Arabic, all of which spoke to her ability to relate to everyone in the office.

"Check it out," she winked, pointing to the memo, twirling out the door in her ballet flats.

The memo read:

Vacation and sick time are issued in full at the beginning of each year and are replenished immediately, in full, on the 1st of the new year. Vacation time: 30 days a calendar year; Sick time: 21 days a year.

We do not work on the following ministry-approved US Holidays:

New Years Day
Martin Luther King Jr. Day
Memorial Day
Independence day
Labor Day
Veterans Day
Thanksgiving
Christmas Day

On the next page, it continued.

We do not work on the following ministry-approved Kuwaiti Holidays:

National Day
Isra' and Mi'raj
Eid ul-Fitr
Eid ul-Adha

The paycheck was generous, but I stared at the time off. Thirty vacation days, twelve holidays, and twenty-one sick days. A week to properly enjoy the wedding was one thing, but a few years back, this time off would have been everything. Paralyzed by my anxiety and unable to leave my house when I needed a moment to heal, the American workplace only offered enough time to slap a Band-Aid on my hemorrhaging mind.

"I'm losing feeling in my legs," I had shouted into the phone after calling 911 in August 2001 when I was twenty-three years old. Rushing home for a quick lunch break, I had run up four flights of stairs to arrive at my apartment door. Out of breath, I felt a sharp pain and rushed to the bathroom, tearing through my purse looking for my phone, sensing I was about to lose consciousness. "An ambulance is on its way. I'll stay on the line," the dispatcher responded.

Moments later, there was a knock at my doorbell.

"They're here," I said as I peeled myself off the cold tile of the bathroom floor, grabbing my keys. At the front door, a man held up a brown paper bag covering the man's face— no sight of a stretcher or EMT badge. A comforting scent momentarily erased all the pain in my body, immediately rewarding me for taking it in slowly, as my mind escaped to a vision of a Greek god.

"Lunch date?" Tyrone said with a pleased grin, holding up a takeout bag with blue writing, from Olympic Cafe.

"Can you give me a ride?" I asked Tyrone.

Into the phone I said, "Never mind, never mind, I don't need an ambulance. Someone here can drop me off."

"You can gimme a ride, right?" I repeated to Tyrone.

"Always," he said with a grin, unfazed by my display of chaos.

Sitting in the passenger's seat of Tyrone's car, I looked around for a switch to turn off the heat, but it wasn't on. My finger pressed down on the window switch, but the temperature didn't change—the fire inside me was rising, and there was no off button. Tyrone U-turned for the second time, flustered by the urgency of finding the hospital that was only two miles away. "Do you know where you're going?" I asked Tyrone. I had lost control of my mind, and Tyrone couldn't find the way.

I redialed 911. "Hi, I just called," I said to a new dispatcher. "Can you give me directions?" I asked as if I pulled over at a 7-11. "Never mind, never mind," I said, hanging up on the dispatcher. With less than zero patience, I snapped at Tyrone, "Where are you going?"

"It's just around the corner," he said in a comfortable tone while driving in circles. In a hospital bed, I lay strapped to an IV; a sedating concoction pumped through my veins, abating my thoughts. Unable to discern up from down, I wondered why the doctor was asking me to count backward by seven as the numbers flooded my head out of order. A torn curtain outlined the small space, concealing as much as the hospital gown that barely covered a birthmark the size of any remaining dignity. Hearing the grotesque descriptions of the patients lying six inches away on either side of me magnified my suffering, forcing me to repeatedly hit the button strapped to the IV for another dose of the narcotic.

The only bit of privacy was suddenly swept back, causing a ripple effect, showing what was behind the curtain, the vulnerability of everyone in their beds. A man startled me when he entered with his identification badge flipped backward, looking down at his clipboard when he asked, "Are you at risk of hurting yourself?" Wasn't I already? No one else was causing this pain. Wasn't I the only one to blame?

Out of fear, I quickly thought to say, "No." What would they do to me if I said yes? Lock me up somewhere?

"You're going to need to call your insurance. Follow up with someone," the doctor said, scribbling on a stack of paper stapled together on his clipboard. "Sign off here," he said, holding the packet of information open to the last page. "Shows we went over everything."

Signing on the dotted line was more fluid than facing the three words he circled in red ink on the first page, "Anxiety disorder, panic, and agoraphobia." He handed me a prescription from his notepad. "Ativan. It'll get you through the week."

The relief I sought was nowhere to be found. I wanted to escape, to go home and get into my bed with a warm blanket to cover me from the frigid coldness of the hospital. Everything was now closing in on me so quickly that the space meant to heal no longer had room for me either.

When I got released, it was the beginning of what felt like the end. Only a few hours later, as the benzodiazepines left my bloodstream, I would hear the knock at the door again, but this time it was all in my head. The panic entered on its own, uninvited, grabbing me by the neck. Gasping for air, no words escaped my mouth as my mind screamed for help.

I was on disability leave from work. HR convinced me I had fourteen sick days to get better. "Added bonus, I see twenty hours of vacation time in your account," the representative said eagerly over the phone. I was a ticking time bomb with fourteen days and twenty hours till imploding. I felt like a lost child—alone, unable to make sense of the world, teaching myself that nowhere was safe, feeling like I needed a grownup to stand next to me and hold my hand. I wore the panic like a backpack, shouldering the weight as it came along everywhere I tried to go and anywhere I wanted to be. For years, I knew my place, taking my seat on a mental rollercoaster with my profession along for the ride. My jobs had never afforded me the luxury of time to rest or to heal.

★ ★ ★

With a paycheck signed by Dr. Mohammad in hand, I calculated what I could afford for rent. I needed a roommate, a furnished room, a place no more than five miles from the office or the train station with a month-to-month lease, the maximum amount of time I could mentally commit. Tyrone came up for the weekend to help me secure a place where I wouldn't feel alone in the world. With only one three potential listings to check out, the housing market felt similar to the job market—sparse pickings meant I would have to kill it on the interview portion.

★ ★ ★

"You are scheduled for a performance test, PowerPoint demonstration, and first-round interview on Monday. The test should take no more than two hours. The interview panel consists of seven members from varying departments who will each ask you a list of questions. As part of the performance test, you will be asked to give a sixty minute PowerPoint presentation on an academic topic or project you have specialized in," the email from a university in San Diego read a few weeks after I started working in LA. I had submitted so many applications, I couldn't even remember what the initial job was. My mind couldn't afford to be tested, to take a day off to interview for another job; beyond the roundtrip train ticket, it would cost me my sanity. "The job requires a master's degree, second language preferred, five years of student advising and counseling, and experience living, working, or volunteering in a foreign country. The compensation is expected to be no more than fifteen dollars an hour. Overtime and weekends expected. Please confirm that you are still interested in interviewing."

Universities that spent their time begging our LA office to send students couldn't afford to pay new hires their worth. During the economic crisis, furloughs and freezes were more common than warm greetings from hiring managers who essentially asked, "Are you overqualified and interested in being underpaid?" or "Take what you can get." In a numbers game where too many were playing, the odds of getting a job in San Diego were not in my favor and not worth it now.

★ ★ ★

Two of the three available apartments were not "as advertised." The third option was *my* only option—a stranger I would be sharing the six hundred square foot space with. Trying not to seem desperate, I hoped to appeal to the stunning female, in her thirties, with dark brown skin and shimmering green eyes.

She pulled me aside to show me the second bedroom, whispering, "He can come over from time to time, but don't make it a regular thing," after she let me know I would be the chosen one.

From her frame of reference, I was a nine-to-fiver. From my perspective, she was an actress who made most of her money working at the House of Blues on Sunset in the private members-only area that I didn't even know existed. Our hours were off. I headed to the office while she was sleeping, and I headed home from work while she was working out. She bartended two days a week to earn more than I would working five days a week to barely cover my rent, which was likely covering her entire mortgage. I hadn't heard of any of the shows she bragged about listed on her IMDb, but that was likely because I grew up without watching TV. As an adult, I didn't own one. If I did watch something, my guilty pleasure was any reality show on Bravo, which was putting this actress roommate out of work.

A week later, my suitcase was unpacked in the dresser drawers of the spare room I rented. My only belongings, tucked away, barely showed any evidence that I lived there. My life looked neat and tidy from inside the room: it had everything I needed—except for the life I dreamed of living with Tyrone.

A loud rhythmic knock bounced off the open apartment door. I stepped out of my room to see my roommate dancing over on her tippy toes, as if she transformed into a ballerina, headed towards her partner standing in the door frame. Her fake lashes covered in dark black mascara were heavier than the soft, rose-colored, silk slip dress dangling on her body.

With my contact lenses drying my eyes out, I blinked hard to see the man she swooned over. But her date just looked like an average sized white male, dressed in cargo shorts and a polo shirt. A short thin leather cord wrapped around his neck with a wood fishhook charm dangled over his hairy chest. The typical LA guy looked dull next to my shimmering roommate.

"This is Jeff," she said with a giant grin and raised eyebrows.

"Hey," I said, heading to the kitchen, with more interest in a snack than an introduction to her flavor of the month. My roommate stared back at me, looking for more of a response, waiting with bated breath for me to coo over the guy. He looked at her and then back at me, waiting. "Have fun?" I said, guessing they wanted a proper send off. She rolled her eyes while trying not to knock off her fake eyelashes. Her look turned from pride to annoyance when I didn't recognize him as the host of *Survivor* and Hollywood celebrity Jeff Probst.

Chapter 7

Income And Outcome

*A*t lunchtime, Liz and I grabbed a bistro table for two in the courtyard. My lunch took up the bistro table where aspiring talents "do lunch" by sipping through straws to slowly fill up on skinny iced lattes. I pulled out my dish of boiled potatoes, green beans, tuna, and hard-boiled eggs dressed in a sweet olive oil dressing.

"*Une petite salade niçoise?*" Liz asked.

"*Oui, oui,*" I replied, "You know my mom studied abroad in Paris, right? In the sixties.

"Cool—my dad's side was there in the sixties too."

"You think at the same time?"

"Probably not."

My eyebrows narrowed.

"My family was there in the 1860s."

Liz's great-great-grandfather initiated what would become a powerful family legacy of dual degree college and medical school graduates from Yale who added studying overseas for additional training to their curriculum vitae long before it was in vogue. Liz was the fifth generation on her family's path. However, after college graduation, she took a detour to head west.

"Was that a lot of pressure?" I asked.

"*Oui, oui*," she grinned.

Back at my desk after lunch, per usual, the phone rang off the hook. The boys, unwilling to wait for more than three rings, were unable to be pacified by anything other than the immediate attention. Not answering rapidly sent them, like a toddler, into a self-entitled tailspin. They were unfamiliar with their demands being met with the boundaries I worked to maintain.

"Miss Jessica?" I heard a soft voice ask over the phone. "I'm calling about Abdullah," she paused, allowing me time to think about which of the seventy-five Abdullahs in my caseload she was referring to. "You helped him," she paused again. "You helped him get into NAU."

"Oh yeah, Abdullah," I said, pegging her as a relative of Abdullah Al Obaid.

"*Shukran*, Miss Jessica," she thanked me. "*Shukran*."

"No problem."

"No, no. I can stay because of you."

"I'm sorry?" I asked, trying to fill in the blanks.

"I'm Abdullah's sister, Amani Al Obaid. Without my brother, I couldn't stay. My father wouldn't let me study." The first call of gratitude came from a female, thanking me for the opportunity I got for her brother. It was the first voice I heard of a female student. There were so few, they had gone unnoticed. I had a lot to learn about the five females out of every one hundred males that were awarded scholarships.

Inside her student file, I found her top scores, her high grades, and her acceptance into five of the schools she applied to. Her brother's file showed twenty-five college applications and the one offer I negotiated.

"My friend, Danah, at UCLA. She's desperate.... Her father. He wants her to return to Kuwait," she paused. "Can she call you? You're our only hope."

After hanging up the phone, I Googled "popular Arab names for females" and then searched my cabinets, which were filled to the brim with hundreds of files for the boys whose cases were overflowing with requests. I pulled out four files to see what else I could learn.

"You're going to need this," Liz said, standing in the door frame. Her back blocked any eyes from seeing a ziplock in her hand, filled with nibbles: "Special batch." She opened a crack of the bag as I breathed in as much of the smell as I could, calming my body as I took a whiff before she tucked it away in my desk drawer. "Just for you," she said. "I'll get you more," she winked, tucking her homemade chocolate chip shortbread into my desk drawer.

Inside our office doors, the females went unnoticed, while outside our building, women were dying to be discovered.

After hours of sitting all day, without making a dent in my work, I packed up for the day, creating a plan to get my body moving. "It's *the* place to be seen," my roommate, who modeled athleisure wear in her spare time, said, convincing me to check out her gym in West Hollywood.

I inched my way down Sunset Boulevard, where the billboards of skinny bodies in skimpy clothes likely motivated others while I sat fully covered eating a Luna bar. I pulled up to the front of the gym, waiting in line behind an idling

Maserati. Welcomed by a sign out on the curb that read, "valet only," I thought, *I'm not paying thirty dollars to park my Honda.* Without any money on me, I circled the block in the bumper-to-bumper traffic, looking for an open metered space, where I would pay the price if I got a ticket. After an hour of going no-where and finishing off a second Luna bar, I decided I couldn't afford to waste my time.

Back at the apartment, I sat on the bed in my rented room, eating a bag of Doritos, trying to keep from staining my roommates' sheets bright orange. I licked my fingers while typing on my computer, mapping out a better plan to get to the gym. I'd have to drive home from work, find a parking spot at my house, and then walk to the gym, where I could then exercise. Feeling motivated, I moved to the couch in the shared space to watch MTV's *The Challenge* after deciding I'd try out my plan the next day. Watching the reality stars pull their body weight up unknotted ropes to play chicken against their opponent over a giant mud pit, I lay down, done with the day, wondering what I was going to have for dinner.

With the slogan "No judgment," Crunch Fitness seemed right up my alley until I entered the front door the next day after work. Parking at my apartment and walking the mile and a half to get there already felt like a workout. Inside, a live DJ spun records at 6 p.m. on a Wednesday. The gym on Sunset Boulevard was filled with people looking like they paid top dollar for their sculpted bodies, showing off the enhancements with high-end gym clothes that barely covered a few bits. Meanwhile, I was wearing sweatpants and an old t-shirt, sitting on a stationary bike, getting nowhere. I didn't have to look in the mirror to know that along with my clothes, this was not a good fit.

Sitting idle on the stationary bike, my heart raced as a text message from Tyrone came through. "Running home to grab a bite. Wish it was with you."

I could hear his voice come through in the message, in just a few words, reminding me that in the busy city where I sat alone, his love was by my side. Never needing a perfect reply, I typed "Ditto." Just honest answers between us, nothing to read between the lines.

"I'm headed out," my roommate said back at the apartment, dressed in a teal ball gown, walking barefoot on her tippy toes. With a Jimmy Choo crystal cocktail clutch, she held the train of her dress in her hand, keeping it from dusting the hardwood floors. "Don't want to leave a mark," she said with her gold stiletto bejeweled Christian Louboutin heels dangling from her wrist like an ornament. While I wondered if her ensemble cost more than I got paid working a whole month, she grabbed the car keys to her Toyota Camry, testing to see if they would fit in her clutch.

"Isn't Jeff picking you up?" I asked, wondering if I would get a glimpse of the pair before TMZ captured a snap with her Prince Charming and selling the moment for all to see.

"Too busy. Just drivin' on my own." She grinned, just thrilled to be seen.

On the red carpet at the Primetime Emmy Awards, the press captured an image of a picture-perfect couple—my roommate grasping for Jeff's arm while he turned to face the cameras. Her beau was a celebrity for the competitive TV program, but the reality was, love is more than just for show.

Chapter 8

The Rumor Mill

"Put a pacifier in their mouths and let them suck it," Dr. Mohammad said. "Do not let the parents hear their cries." Dr. Mohammad wanted us to calm the students and quell any temper tantrums before hearing about it from a parent whose child wasn't getting their way. The workday consisted of fielding complaints from the male students who made multiple phone calls to whine until they got what they wanted.

Without a pacifier, the boys were quick to tattletale. The fathers, more interested in nepotism than feminism, skipped right over the female advisors, phoning Dr. Mohammad directly. His cell and home phone numbers stood out prominently on the landing page of the office website. Not knowing the code to check his voice messages, a single ring would cue him to answer the call. When the fathers were on the phone, Dr. Mohammad's ego was on the line.

He coddled the students, fearing any news getting back to Kuwait that wasn't good news would cost him everything. Professionally, there was more risk than reward weighing on his shoulders. Success went unnoticed, but failure was tied to his name. Like an audience at a magic show, the Ministry of Higher Education watched closely as Dr. Mohammad was on stage, with the colossal undertaking of establishing our office out of not much more than thin air.

Awaiting responses from the ministry via fax for weeks at a time, we stared at the archaic device, wondering if anyone heard our requests. Gathering around the machine, the advisors caught up on office gossip. We understood speaking disparagingly was against the teaching of the Qur'an, the religious book guiding Muslims who follow Islam, yet the rumor mill in Kuwait was a well-oiled machine. Traveling faster than the speed of light, rumors crossed the ocean and traversed the desert. When they returned to our office just as quickly, we heard there was even a newspaper that highlighted "discrepancies" made by Kuwaiti nationals, which featured a few blunders that took place in our office. To put out a fire, Dr. Mohammad often used fuel.

"Do not speak to them," Dr. Mohammad shouted out down the hallway. "They just want to see us fail," he said in disgust, referring to the embassy in DC. The idealism of working together for the betterment of the students was not realistic.

"Do not speak to them," Dr. Mohammad yelled down the hall again before sending out a follow-up memo to the twelve members of our staff that got the message. As if trying to decipher a fight amongst toddlers, it was unclear who started it. We were no longer allowed to communicate with the DC office. Leaving the poorly behaved leadership with only finger paints, our office was an empty canvas to fill.

The rumor was, as we took on half of their workload, we would be able to hire more staff, and the DC office would have to start layoffs. With everything on the line, Dr. Mohammad held an opportunity to create something from the ground up. But with everything on the line, failure was deemed a fate worse than death.

To accomplish our job, we needed advice on everything. The varying types of scholarship regulations, visas, finances, immigration documents, university policies, and legal matters were just the beginning. We knew better than to shut our office doors to make a secret call to the staff in DC.

Our empty office suite filled with noise; Dr. Mohammad shouted down the halls when he wanted to call an advisor to his office instead of picking up one of the many phones covering his desk. "The doors remain open for all to pass through." It was a rule we all learned to abide by. Closing a door to shut the sound out was unheard of.

"You can't smoke without fires," Dr. Mohammad spewed, unintentionally encouraging me to fire back by taking up smoking. The only way to have a real conversation was to get some fresh air outside of the building. The accountants, Viraj and Abdul Baatin, were already in the courtyard, breaking up their fifteen-hour workday with four minutes to suck in as much smoke as possible every other hour in lieu of lunch. Rapport with our DC counterparts meant survival by smoking. Stepping outside, pretending to be on a smoke break, would be the backdoor approach to calling upon the embassy. I bought a pack of cigarettes and lit one up. Before heading back into the office, we walked back and forth into the smoke as if it was perfume, hoping in the meantime, our office wouldn't go up in flames.

At lunchtime, the elevator doors opened, and the women from our office shuffled inside. Squeezing to turn around, they shrugged in unison seeing Liz and I standing on the outside. "No worries," I said, cuing the women to narrow their eyebrows at my words as the doors closed.

The next elevator to arrive was empty. Liz held her hand out to hold the doors open, and I held my breath, waiting to feel the space drop down.

"Are you ready to talk wedding dresses?" Liz asked.

"Nah." I paused. Relieved by the distraction of my thoughts, "Weird, right?"

"Absolutely not—I'm never getting married," she replied.

"What about William?" Her boyfriend of four years. They lived together in LA and knew each other from back home. They grew up in the same town in Connecticut where the historic homes that lined the streets were as old as the money of the waspy families that occupied them. White fences created a divide between the yards of perfectly man-icured neighbors. A church bell rang through the town on Sunday, calling people to come together in the pews where children were hushed while the adults kept their gossip at a whisper.

"My parents can't stand that we're together."

"Aren't your families friends?"

"My parents think I should marry up. They aren't as rich. One marriage was enough for me anyway."

I narrowed my eyebrows. "One marriage?"

"Growing up with my parents would make anyone stay single for a lifetime."

Chapter 9

Death By Tiramisu

The traffic driving to work down Sunset Boulevard looked like a parking lot, while the sidewalks, which no one used, were blocked by "Valet Only" signs. Larger than life billboards served to distract the drivers. Models advertising all of their skinny body parts were surrounded by sidewalk bistros where posers chilled without eating, hoping to be noticed, while the tourists lined up around the corner to eat hot dogs from a famous stand.

Needing an image that was not in my face, I looked away from the road, reaching for my phone to focus on a distraction. Scrolling through my updates, I saw "Fatema will be twenty-eight today." The only thing worse than a birthday surprise at work was no one remembering at all. If I made it through the stoplights in fifty-five minutes, a stop at Vons to grab a cake would only cost twenty more minutes. Adding it all up, I'd only be fifteen additional minutes later than my usual fifteen minutes late. Three months into the job, I knew we ran on Kuwaiti time, translating "arriving on time" into "early" and "a little late" into "on time."

At the grocery store, I looked to see what was on display in the dessert case. The dark contrasting colors, the sweet smell awakening the senses, the swirls of chocolate—the perfect ingredients. There were two things that bridged the divide in our office: coffee and dessert. "I'll take the tiramisu." Getting everyone on the same page, bringing us all together, to share in a moment of celebration, would be the icing on the cake. Unlike everything else in our office, confections were the one way you could do no wrong.

Arriving at work, I held my breath for the elevator ride up, as if capturing the air to blow out all the candles. My body temperature rising on the ride up, I tried to keep myself steady, preventing the cake from sliding out of my sweaty palms.

"*Yaneh*, a feast for eyes," Hala said as I stepped into the office suite. Relieved, I grinned with glee, knowing this would make a Jewish mother proud—remembering to celebrate, to make someone feel special. "Put it with the others," she said.

The others?

Like schoolgirls, we waited for the lunch bell to ring. In the empty space between all of the offices, a table dressed up for the occasion lined with a buffet of desserts from all the staffers who believed everyone forgot Fatema's birthday. Liz's shortbread, Nahla's flan, and Hala's baklava awakened the senses without coffee. Nubia brought *feteer meshaltet*, layers of pastry dough. The ghee in between each layer is what gave the butter-like substance a nutty flavor. The spices of our lives added more color than any frosted sheet cake ever could.

Dina made her family recipe of *basbousa* for everyone to try. The Egyptian semolina cake made with yogurt, honey, and coconut was soft on the tongue. Drizzled with simple syrup, the cake was adorned with pistachios around the circumference and one almond sliver on each piece. The bottom was perfectly browned from the tahini and ghee used in lieu of buttering the pan. More impressive than the taste was the cut of each piece, pre-sliced with a precision I had never seen before. Still in the round pan, slices created individual diamond servings that formed a star in the center. The perfectly cut diamonds were handed out first, leaving the rough-cut diamonds for those who arrived late. Dina and Nubia debated semolina versus farina while I savored all the flavors new to my tongue.

The tiramisu was removed from the front of the dessert line and replaced at the end to be served last after all of the other cakes had been eaten and there was nothing left to choose. The label from the grocery store put it in its place, alerting the others that it was not homemade, lacking the authentic flavor of sweat and tears. Like a scarf slightly fallen out of place on a devout Muslim woman, showing the nape of her neck—revealing more than intended, eyes glanced away, not showing any interest in looking at it.

"*Yaneh*, know your place," Nubia snapped at the only men in our office, the two accountants and the chauffeur, pointing to the end of the line, while Hala gave them the evil eye. "*Shukran, habibi*," Hala said over her shoulder, arms crossed, returning her gaze to wink at Nubia. When the two women stood their ground, the men understood to take the cue to step aside. With exaggerated force, they turned their backs to the men standing in the room. The two divorcées stood unwavering, united in their stance, the strength in their voices coming through loud and clear. Unlike their marriages, they did not submissively step into the background until they went unnoticed. In so many places these two women had kept their mouths shut—but not here—not now. Nubia and Hala served each other while the men waited in the back of the room until all of the other women helped themselves. Dina was third in line, putting two large servings on her plate. When she swirled around on her ballet flats to grab a fork, her untucked blouse swayed the opposite way, momentarily revealing a thin hair tie looped to hold her unfastened button to the buttonhole, an inch of her zipper undone. The shirt covered the news that Dr. Mohammad was not expecting.

The homemade treats devoured immediately left the cake from Vons for the men to share.

"Oh Jessica Keith, what is that delight?" Abdul Baatin smiled at me, acknowledging my effort, unlike the others from the back of the room.

"Tiramisu," I said as he approached the table. His gaunt frame stood out even more, now that he was no longer hiding behind his desk, head down with his calculator, or smoking in the courtyard. His pants were held onto his body by a belt wrapped nearly twice around his waist, holding up his oversized pants. "Let me cut you a piece," I said, slicing an exaggeratedly large serving, like a Jewish mother, just wanting to cure his woes with a plate of food.

From the corner of the room, Nahla's usual scoff took me by surprise. She darted towards Abdul Baatin, like a wild bull entering the ring at a rodeo, lunging at him while shouting, "What's wrong with you?" Smacking his plate with so much force, I thought his fragile frame might collapse to the floor, along with his cake that was now face down on the carpet.

After shoving through the crowd, she fixed her glance at me, mouthing something I couldn't translate.

He can have coffee, I reassured myself, *I've seen him drink coffee. I've seen him by the coffee maker and at Starbucks. He can have coffee*, I repeated, convincing myself that I wasn't in the wrong.

Staring at me, Nahla mouthed, "You idiot."

Oh, my goodness. The ladyfingers. He can't lick the icing off the ladyfingers. Can he not eat ladyfingers? It's not a real lady? I sighed, frustrated, not understanding how I read this wrong.

"There's alcohol in it, you idiot," Nahla scoffed.

Everyone gawked at the dessert that now no one would touch, as I wondered why I was feeling such disappointment over a store-bought cake that no one wanted anything to do with.

★ ★ ★

The following week, I tested out a theory: biking the five miles to work was a better use of my time than sitting in traffic. I headed down Sunset Boulevard as the sun broke through the gray skies filled with clouds of smog. Rusty as the brakes on the ride Liz lent me, I carried a backpack with my bottles of pills tucked below my work clothes and makeup.

Hotels peppered the street between Chateau Marmont and the Viper Room, where the only people walking looked to service a client driving by. Meanwhile, the valet escorted businessmen discreetly into cars that hightailed it out of the hotel driveways without looking, straight into the bumper-to-bumper traffic. Undetected by the car racing through the hotel's driveway, I clenched the hand brakes, cueing the bike to come to an abrupt stop; my body flung forward, and my ribs slammed against the handlebars, then jerking back down into the narrow seat.

"Whadaya think you're doin?" a man in a tailored suit matching the awning of the hotel shouted at me, moving a "valet only" stanchion onto the sidewalk.

Trying not to die, I thought.

"Get outta here…" he yelled, brushing his hand fiercely in the air. He shooed me away like a transient, more concerned with the sidewalk real estate diminishing than the value of the lives who crossed its path.

Barely unscathed by the ride, arriving to work alive felt nothing short of a miracle. In the basement of our office building, I locked Liz's bike up to an empty rack surrounded by high-end luxury vehicles. In the lobby bathroom, I changed like Superman in a stall, hovering over the toilet, trying not to let my blouse sleeve take a dip in the toilet bowl. At the sink, I splashed some water on my face and took an assessment of my reflection in the mirror. With sweat dripping down my face, I decided against foundation. Waiting in line for the elevator, I threw some lipstick on to match my beet-red cheeks as I wiped the sweat off my forehead with my dirty gym shirt. While other women clutched their pearls, I threw my backpack over my shoulder, stepping into the death trap. Even unnoticed, I stood out.

"Another cook in the kitchen to stir the pot." Nubia translated into the rumor mill. "There's going to be a new sheriff in town," Nubia cackled. "Flying another cultural attaché from Kuwait to command our office." Dr. Mohammad's theories convinced us to believe DC sent the message overseas to Kuwait. It was true, though: our office needed help. We were barely treading water. With oversized caseloads and limited staffing, we were overworked and outnumbered, desperate for approvals from the ministry to offer relief.

"A spy," Dr. Mohammad hissed at Ashley. "They are sending us a spy." Nothing was announced to the staff, alerting us to any chain of command. Instead, we relied on the rumors we discussed, pretending to be on a smoke break. "He thinks the other cultural attaché is coming to sabotage us," Ashley explained outside, where we all stood taking turns to walk through the smoke. "Dr. Mohammad has no intention of sharing his position."

A corner office, a place of prestige, was prepared for the incoming diplomat. However, the leaders would be sitting in the two opposing sides of the ring. Dr. Mohammad and the advisors were on one end, and the distressed accountants and chauffeur were on the other end. The second cultural attaché would arrive in July, three months before my wedding. We knew the new leader was a person of power, a high ranking official with years of experience, a PhD in statistics, and chosen by the Ministry of Higher Education and members of the Parliament.

Everyone arrived to work on time for the big day. "Did you see Dr. Mohammad's wife?" I instant messaged Liz. "Is this like a first lady thing?" We never met Dr. Mohammad's wife. Despite his jokes about multiple wives, we knew he only married one. He never spoke of his family—to him, it was like selling them out to the tabloids.

"Are you inviting them to your wedding?" Liz messaged back.

"Undecided," I replied.

I heard the smacking of Nahla's gum as she walked by my office door.

"Hey, did you meet her?" I asked Nahla.

"Yeah. And?"

"What did she say?"

"She didn't say anything."

"Does his wife speak English?"

Nahla rolled her eyes, "That's not his wife. That's the new cultural attaché."

From all of the details I gathered, I neglected to add up that the cultural attaché would be, most surprisingly, a woman.

From far away, she appeared to be middle-aged and boxy, wearing layers of clothing covering her from head to toe. A full length long-sleeved dress on top of a turtleneck, with a scarf wrapped a few times around her head and neck, left only her hands and face uncovered.

There were no formal introductions. No welcoming.

At lunchtime, Liz and I waited for the elevator, whispering to each other. "Did you see *the enemy*?" Liz giggled. "I heard she came with her daughters, leaving her husband back in Kuwait,"

"Did you talk to her?" I asked.

"No. You?"

"No. Dr. Mohammad would freak out if he saw us talking." I laughed out loud.

"*Marhaban*," an unfamiliar voice interrupted us from behind.

Dr. Saamia approached us as we waited for the elevator—the curly-haired Jew-fro and sidekick, the two most obvious Americans. She greeted us in Arabic.

I froze. Then bowed. Then raised my hand as if to show I come in peace. *What am I doing?* I had no idea how to greet the cultural attaché.

The door to the elevator opened. We stepped to the side to let Dr. Saamia enter first and then scurried behind her in the tight space, with the walls closing in on us.

She stood inches away, facing the closed doors, not saying a word, while Liz and I mouthed to each other behind her back. Getting a closer look, I was surprised by the details of her covered body. The billowing square cut fabric was animal print, the long sleeves wrapped with sparkling bracelets. A French manicure was inconspicuous against a scarf, the word Gucci swirled into the design, tied tightly around her head. In a hot city like LA, you could peg her as an Arab cougar.

★ ★ ★

"Do you think my daughter's a whore?" the father yelled into the phone at Dr. Mohammad. "Do you want her working the streets?" The man demanded answers when his daughter's monthly salary was put on hold when she failed to submit her verification of enrollment, one of the few requirements of the scholarship. He knew this regulation due to his high rank in the ministry. I knew four of his five children—all of the boys were attending US colleges on their own scholarships. An Audi dealership contacted me for verification of funds when the four boys went together, each applying to lease a ride to get to campus from their furnished apartments with doormen, a few miles away from where other students tripled up in dorms.

"My daughter is not a whore," the father yelled through the phone, "How do you expect her to pay rent?" he demanded.

"Please, please," Dr. Mohammad mouthed for help, calling me over, waving his arms frantically. Dr. Mohammad pleaded in Arabic for forgiveness, giving the father lip service,

while I was forced to lip read, "Release her. Release her."
He looked down at his desk, ripped off the corner of a piece
of paper and scribbled down the name Aisha Al Abudullah.

"Her salary?" Dr. Mohammad looked at me, hand covering the mouthpiece on the phone, "How do you get it released
immediately?" he asked me. "You're my only..." he stopped
himself, noticing three other advisors on approach.

Aisha's case was managed by Holly, a twenty-something
brunette who was in her second week on the job. Until she passed
the three-month trial period, she was called "the new hire."

Her first mistake was misunderstanding the government
regulation "hold the salary for students who did not have
proof of enrollment."

"Just a heads up," I grin to reassure her, "rules apply to
everyone, just sporadically." She stood with me as I asked
Abdul Baatin, "Can we expedite a one-time wire transfer?
Six thousand dollars to Aisha Al Abdullah's account?" I ran
her through the official process of just getting it done.

Abdul Baatin looked up from his ruler, guiding the lines
on the bank documents he printed out in a large font. "Right
away," he said with a grin.

Back at my desk, the phone rang. "Hello, Miss Jessica?
Please help," I heard a girl's voice come through the line.

"Hello?" I replied.

"The school says I have to live in the dorm. Freshman re-
quirement. My father says I can't go if I have to live like them."

"I'm so sorry," I said, "Who's this calling?"

"Liah Al Abdani."

I looked at my list of students, reconfiguring her last
name, spelling it every different way. "I'm just looking at

my list…" I said to the girl, continuing to scroll through the names.

"I'm not on a list," she said. "My friend Dahlia said you know how to help. You're my only hope."

★ ★ ★

Tyrone stayed late at work on Friday to avoid rush hour, making the drive up to LA in only two and a half hours after a ten-hour day. Too tired to do anything that night, I planned an evening out for the two of us on Saturday. My roommate recommended a restaurant she described as "*the* place to go." We parked a few blocks away from the commerce and chaos on the main street and enjoyed the evening hand in hand, strolling down a tree lined street in the neighborhood of Beverly Grove.

Three older men walked on the other side of the street with four little boys following them like baby chicks. The men dressed in long black coats and large brimmed black hats. Their dark, thick beards blended into their jackets, but two curls stood out, framing both sides of their faces. The little boys wore the same outfits as the men but with kippot on their heads, and without the beards, their two curls resembled pigtails.

I rubbed my thumb on the inside of Tyrone's hand. His smile met mine.

Outside of the restaurant, The Little Door, a hostess blocked the entryway. The woman stood tall behind her station in black combat boots. Her short black sequin dress peeked out from a wool red trench coat adorned with gold epaulets. A table for four dressed to the nines walked right past us through the ten foot imported wood doors.

"Reservation?" the hostess asked without looking up from her notepad, unimpressed at my response of "We need one?"

"We can seat you at eleven," she replied.

"P.m.?" I responded, squinting at her reaction. She looked unfazed, standing at command in front of the French restaurant, resembling a guard of the coveted seats, when all I wanted was to sit down, undetected, just anywhere next to Tyrone.

A few shops down, we found a cozy marketplace, Joan's on Third. A basket filled with freshly baked French bread was on display next to an overflowing cheese case. Desserts were showcased like jewelry behind sparkling glass cases with labels to entice the consumer. Cloud cupcakes with chocolate-dipped marshmallow icing swirled perfectly next to the chocolate roulade, crown cake, and a kouign-amann, a dessert similar to a puff pastry, shining from the layers of butter. The sweet goods showed off their status resting on pedestal platters. My eyes were unable to look away. "Just dessert?" I suggest in lieu of dinner that evening.

"One problem," Tyrone said through a smile. "I don't see any tiramisu."

Chapter 10

Scholarships On Ice

"*D*r. Mohammad will die." In a hushed voice, I repeated to Hala, "He'll die." I peeked out the door to see if anyone was walking by. "If he finds out, we'll all get fired."

Dr. Saamia committed her first error behind Dr. Mohammad's back. She invited all of the female staffers over for tea on a Sunday afternoon at her house in Beverly Hills.

"What if we ask for Dr. Mohammad's permission?" Hala asked me.

"Maybe? You mean, ask Dr. Saamia to ask Dr. Mohammad if we can go to her house?" I replied.

Popping up on instant messenger, I see "Coffee?" from Liz. "Meet in basement Starbucks."

"Yeah—go ask Dr. Saamia," I said to Hala, sending her on a mission.

At the elevator, the doors opened just in time to escape one conversation yet trapped me with the voice in my head. As I glanced around, I could see my fear reflected in the mirrored walls. I diverted my eyes to search for a secret compartment or trap door, as if I was in a magic show. The penetrating heat from the spotlight blinded me from seeing my life flash by. The steel and glass made the space heat up at an exponential rate. As my senses were heightened, my reality became sharp with clarity: I was aware that there were cameras hidden behind the glass. I couldn't decide what would be worse—that we were under surveillance with some guy and his cup of coffee, sitting back watching this shitshow, or that no one was watching—as the cameras kept rolling, capturing everything without anyone noticing. My limp body now struggled to stand, eyes to the ground, wanting no one to notice me. I waited to feel a plunge, hoping it wasn't coming from my body.

The thrill of surviving the ride made it feel worthwhile until I was here again. The adrenaline that tricked me into playing, exhausting every bit of me, temporarily erased my mind as it left my abandoned body. While each time would be different, every time I was taking a risk. There would be new, unfamiliar faces around me, unknowing participants. I would hope for them that today wasn't the day.

My short-lived self-assurance was stifled by my mind trying to create a mathematical equation of my life's expectancy. If chance is fifty-fifty, when does luck run out? My endurance wrestled with the strong-willed thought that I may be accelerating the likelihood of my own death, pinned down by my mind. My helpless physical self couldn't fight the effort it took to separate from my mind. They were stuck together without any way to escape. I lost control. Even surprised by a win, I still felt like I lost—every time, I chose to bet against myself.

A ding from my phone, alerting me of a new text, brought me back to reality. The message from Hala read, "Didn't go well. Her response = don't come if u r afraid."

★ ★ ★

"They left me to die," Mohammad said over the phone. "A prisoner in a cage."

I listened intently to the student just released from Immigration and Customs Enforcement (ICE).

"No food. I starved in the darkness," his voice shook. "I didn't know what they were going to do to me."

His file showed he had completed three years at a university in Washington with a 3.5 GPA.

"I'll go home," he pleaded with the officers. "I'll stay away."

Mohammad was stopped at customs and taken to secondary inspection. "I should have picked a different line," he said, as if it was his fault, describing the angst of the officer's glare before Mohammad had even shown him his passport.

"They confiscated my cell and my laptop, reviewing my recent searches."

"Mohammad," I sighed, hoping my empathy was received on the other end of the line.

Mohammad was taken away in handcuffs, and sent to immigration detention, from his port of entry, LA, for having WhatsApp, an instant messaging platform, on his phone. Tracking his location, for his parents to communicate with him upon his arrival at the airport ensuring he made it safely.

"I lost everything," he said, referring to his laptop, cell phone, and luggage filled with all of his belongings. A one-way ticket home bought him out of detainment. In lieu of defending himself, he chose to leave everything behind.

"It can all be replaced," I said, knowing the worst of what he lost was his final year needed to complete his degree.

Chapter 11

Letting Our Hair Down

"*S*halom y'all," etched into a piece of wood, painted in cheerful colors, hung off a rusted nail right above the doorbell, and just below it was a mezuzah. *She lives in a Jewish home?* I thought, arriving at the doorpost of Dr. Saamia's house.

While Dr. Mohammad finding out was daunting, a glimpse inside a real Beverly Hills mansion was too tantalizing to pass up. The palm tree-lined street was the grand entrance into the exclusive neighborhood where the Kuwaiti government rented Dr. Saamia's Spanish revival house for $25,000 a month. I pulled up in my Honda, carefully reading the parking signs, hoping I wouldn't get a ticket for my dirty car not belonging to this pristine neighborhood.

The door swung open before I could even ring the bell. My grin met by a stranger. A young woman with long black silky hair, wearing a bright red low cut dress cinched at the waist with matching bright red lipstick, said, "Come on in."

Her staff's allowed to wear that? Isn't that a bit much for a Sunday? I was fully clothed in denim slacks and a long-sleeved sweater. I assumed an outfit appropriate for work would be sufficient as a guest. The woman directed me with her bare arm to point me in the direction of the women from the office, who were all grinning back at me. I squeezed onto the couch next to Liz. "Do you believe that?" she asked.

"I know, right?" I replied, not needing to say, "Do you believe her staff dresses like that?"

Liz nudged me with her elbow.

"What?" I mouth, shrugging my shoulders. Her eyes widen, and her head tilts towards the woman in the red dress. I squinted to decipher her message. The woman in red smiled, twirling around, waiting for me to notice, as Liz whispers, "That *is* Dr. Saamia."

The beautiful woman looked ten years younger and ten pounds lighter without the layers of clothes covering her figure. She let her silky, black hair sway around while we all snacked on sweets, danced, and smoked hookah. A week ago, when I asked Dr. Saamia, "Should Tyrone come?" she replied, "Without men there, the women can let their hair down."

Unlike Dr. Saamia's hair, typically wrapped in a scarf, veiling her true self, my Jew-fro stood out like a badge, identifying me to my tribe. The last time I sat in a salon chair, my world was spinning, optimistic that getting my hair relaxed would have a domino effect on the rest of my body. My ears filled with the sound of the water cascading in the background as the hairdresser ran her hands through my hair.

"What kind of damage are we doing today?"

The big, curly, frizzy hair was the only part of me that I thought I was capable of controlling. But it was more like squeezing myself into a tight pair of Spanx—trying to force a part of myself to be something I wasn't. She began splitting my hair into sections as she painted the relaxer onto the roots. Her assistant rubbed Frankincense oil into the palm of my hands, focusing on the pressure points.

"This relieves internal obstruction, allowing a flow of energy through your body." She placed heated gloves over the hot oils. "It's *the* solution for reversing time—only select salons carry it." I closed my eyes to avoid them from revealing my skepticism, waiting for the magical potion to take me back to a time where I didn't need the meds that kept me alive without moving forward.

"It just needs to stay in for like fifteen minutes," the hairdresser noted, hitting the clamp on the chair, plunging me backward. Setting the timer, she flipped the switch, signaling my cue to feel trapped in a straightjacket, desperate to bust out like Houdini, surrounded by smoke and mirrors. With the amplified sound of the running water and my neck flung back off the chair, it felt like I was being waterboarded in a funhouse, gasping for air with a distorted perception as the others laughed.

"Get it out," I screamed with desperation at the stylist to remove the chemical out of my hair before I jumped out of my skin. *I'm on fire.* "Get it out," I pleaded, unable to help myself as my head spins in circles. The chemicals scorched my thoughts as the air blowing around me fanned the flames, causing the burning sensation ablaze throughout my body. The room filled with women just stared, craning their necks, curious to get a glimpse as if parked near a horrible accident but unwilling to take any action that might chip a nail.

It would have been easier to be on fire; the pain I felt was invisible to the world. No words could explain what was happening to my body as it was being tortured by my mind. Once it shut the trap door, there was no escaping—it didn't matter where I was or what I was doing. Fifteen minutes sitting in a chair was too much; my thoughts paralyzed my body as they screamed, "Danger, danger, get out!" Running out of the salon into the car, my wet hair dripped onto my white shirt, revealing more of myself than I was ready to see.

I called Tyrone. "Hey, how's it goin'?" he answered.

"You there?" I asked, "Can ya talk a sec?"

"Isn't that what we're doing?" I could feel his smile over the phone. His words resuscitated my mind, breathing life back into me. At times, it felt like a window seat looking out at the ocean during a prison sentence. The view changed my perspective, but ultimately, I was still confined, unable to escape. The person I couldn't even recognize in the mirror would see Tyrone's greatest downfall as having fallen in love with someone who wasn't me.

Chapter 12

What'd Jew Say?

"It's not like we're getting married," I said to my mother before my first date with Tyrone in April 2001. "But no, he's not Jewish," is all she heard. The rest didn't matter. The only message was a nagging lecture about the importance of having a Jewish family. My mother's voice was a ringing noise in my ear. I couldn't pacify it, and it ruminated so loudly in my head that I wrongly assumed Tyrone could hear it too while we sat at dinner. But even the cry of a Jewish woman ranting didn't rattle him when I blurted out on our first date, "I'm having Jewish babies."

My mother's side of the family came from a long line of Orthodox Jewish rabbis for generations until my great-great-grandfather made a startling decision. He converted. Although it was only a transition to Reform Judaism, a more modern take on the religion, the differences within the same religion shattered the family. He would be the last known rabbi in our lineage.

I checked every box for Jewish milestones. From birth to bat mitzvah, a Jewish wedding was next.

"Are you inviting Dr. Mohammad?" my mother asked, reviewing her to-do list.

"Undecided."

"Have you gotten Rabbi Bernstein's approval yet?" she asked.

For the traditional Jewish wedding we were planning, we needed the ceremony performed by a rabbi who gave us his blessing. But not just any rabbi. The rabbi from my grandparents' temple in Memphis, Tennessee—a city in the south that made a visit in 2000 feel like traveling back in time to a town in the 1960s.

My family put all of their faith in Rabbi Bernstein. Ordained in 1964, he came from a long line of rabbis. More significant for my family though, was that he performed my parents' wedding in 1973, my sister's wedding in 2003, my grandfather's bar mitzvah in 1986 at the age of seventy-five, and his funeral in 1987 at the age of seventy-six. The rabbi's approval meant a commitment to living Jewishly.

I believed that Tyrone was my beshert—it was written in our book of life that we would find each other, meeting at the crossroads of destiny and faith. Our love so patient, it waited until this lifetime to have the opportunity to just be together in a most authentic way. A true love born at its time. It didn't need anyone's approval. Until now. We needed Rabbi Bernstein's blessing to perform the ceremony.

When the rabbi at my family's congregation in Albuquerque, New Mexico, heard we were getting married, he made his beliefs clear. "Interfaith marriages? I don't believe in them," he said to my mother, "but I am willing to be a guest."

"He's not welcome at the wedding," I said to my mother.

"I'm on the board. What am I supposed to tell him?" she asked.

"He's not welcome," I repeated, using my voice to stand my ground, knowing I was in quicksand. I didn't dare bring up the seat at the table, saved for a guest we both knew would speak up against the wedding.

★ ★ ★

"Are you on the list?" I asked the admissions counselor, sounding like a bouncer at a nightclub that everyone wanted to get into. In LA, there was always a list—a city filled with membership only bars, hidden speakeasies, and restaurants that thrived as invite-only.

Our office was no different. I pulled out my reference sheet to see if Santa Monica Community College was on the list of approved universities.

"No, I'm sorry. I don't see you on the list."

The over-eager college representative asked, "How do I get on?" salivating for any inside information.

"I'm sorry," I said, unremorseful. The list of names was set—she had no chance of getting in. Trying to stop the conversation in its tracks, I saw a red light flashing, another caller trying to get through. "Can I get back to you?" I left the conversation hanging, unable to hear the response, uncoiling the cord to the phone that was ringing off the hook.

"Thanks for getting back to me right away," I said to the admissions counselor at Northern Arizona University. "I was wondering if you could take another look at Abdullah Al

Obaid's application," I asked, referring to the son of a friend of Dr. Mohammad's whose low GPA and barely cutting it English test scores denied him everywhere else he applied. "Dr. Mohammad would be thrilled to send more students there," I said, knowing the counselor would only hear the sound of a winning slot machine.

Even when the US is unwelcoming to foreigners, universities saw big dollar signs for international students who paid full price admission and are required to show bank statements with tens of thousands of dollars in liquid funds available to receive consideration for their visas. Knowing the Kuwaiti government footed the bill, schools didn't have to recruit individuals one by one. They were just a phone call away from receiving dozens of students at a time based on the quality of their program and their relationship with Dr. Mohammad.

The next call I switched over to was the voice of a young male, his voice cracking, "Hello, Miss Jessica. It's Ahmed. How is your family?" he asked, the typical greeting used before any request.

"I'm calling to change my major to economics."

"You know you have to stay with your decreed major, right?"

"I don't understand any of my classes," he said, his voice cracking again.

Away from his family, in the US for the first time, he was alone in an unfamiliar new world. With no other Kuwaitis accepted at Stanford, he was engulfed by fourth-generation alumni bragging about their legacies as they sat around a TV in the common area of a coed dorm eating pepperoni pizza, talking about getting smashed at ragers.

"I'm sorry," I said, knowing he's seventeen years old, his future assigned by the ministry with the major of petroleum engineering. "Have you talked with your father?" I asked, both of us understanding it's not for advice—it's for his Rolodex. "Do you have any family working at the ministry?" I asked, knowing that nepotism in the US translates in Arabic as "*wasta*," the unofficial official way to make change. Knowing a guy who knows a guy got you further than patience or going by the book. I remembered seeing a T-shirt that said, "Keep Calm Cause I Have Wasta."

The call was interrupted by a smell filling the office. "Can I get back to you?" I asked, hoping he knew to translate that to "goodbye."

The scent of a shirt covered in a bottle of Dolce and Gabbana cologne alerted me that an eighteen-year-old student sat in the conference room, likely wearing an Abercrombie and Fitch rugby shirt.

"Nubia, we got a fresh one. Can you help bring 'em in?" I asked, peeking my head into her workspace.

"*Salam*, Mohammad. I'm going to review the scholarship regulations with you," I said, pausing so Nubia could translate into Arabic.

Sentence by sentence, we spent two hours with every student explaining their requirements. Some messages they got right away: "You will receive a monthly allowance, a book allowance, a clothing allowance..." I said to the student who lacked experience using an ATM, opening a bank account, or even pumping gas.

With big payouts, we tried to ensure they understood, "You are required to send us your verification of enrollment at the beginning of the semester," to show they were signed up for the appropriate classes, "and your transcript at the end of each semester," to assess their outcome of the term.

"Provided you maintain a GPA of 2.8, you'll be awarded a ticket home at the end of each academic year," I said, pained that the students received bonuses.

Since the government was dishing out so much, they ensured the students understood what they were required to fork over. "If you fail to complete your degree, you are required to pay back the Kuwaiti government the price of tuition, salary, and all bonuses received over the entire time you were in the US. Is that clear?" I asked the student whose blank stare waited for Nubia to translate the sentence into some sort of motherly advice. Meanwhile, I was doing the mental calculations of what the student would owe if he didn't finish his degree. Average tuition of $30,000 per year plus $2,700 a month stipend plus $700 book allowance plus $600 clothing allowance plus $1,400 airplane tickets plus any additional bonuses. All multiplied by the number of years completed.

The majority of the students still needed an acceptance to college. They came to the US a year in advance, covered in full by the government, to study English, needing to pass university language requirements before being officially admitted. I tacked on the additional cost for the year Mohammad was studying English.

"Any questions?" I asked, knowing he would turn to Nubia and ask her in Arabic where he picked up his first check. I pointed my finger to the document, where he signed off that he understood every regulation. Without question, Mohammad scribbled on the document, grabbed his check from Abdul Baatin, and asked Dr. Mohammad's chauffeur to drive him back to his hotel, the Grand Hyatt, located two blocks away. I wondered if this eighteen-year-old student understood that he could owe over half a million dollars if he didn't finish his degree.

Back at my computer, I look up to see Fatema, reaching her hand out, offering me a piece of gum. "That older lady should piss off," she cackled.

"Seriously? Not even trying. She didn't even color her hair." Fatema stuck a piece of gum in her mouth, pointing her head in the direction of an older woman waiting to be interviewed by Dr. Mohammad. She wore a business suit from the '80s with oversized shoulder pads draped over her petite frame, resembling a child playing dress-up in her parents' clothes.

"Surprised they didn't catch that from her resume," she said, chewing away. "I bet he doesn't even meet with her."

"What?" I shook my head.

"No fogies," she replied, chewing away at her gum.

"What'd you say?" I asked.

"No Jews or fogies allowed." Eyes open wide, excited by the size of the bubble she blew with her gum. *Pop*, the bubble burst. "Ugh," she said, disgusted that her gum was stuck to some hair by her mouth; she headed towards the bathroom, leaving me hanging.

My fingers started typing, banging away at the computer, trying to keep up with my racing thoughts. "Talk. Now," I instant messaged Liz.

"Meet in 15?" she replied.

"Now."

"'K, leaving out front door."

I dashed out the back door, not caring if anyone heard it slam behind me.

"What's up?" Liz asked, thirsty for some juicy gossip.

"Fatema just said Jews can't work here."

"Wait a sec," she said, putting her finger to her mouth, pulling me by the hand to the elevator, pressing the down button. "Wait till we're outside," she hushed as if we were being taped.

We stood silently in the elevator surrounded by typical LA business execs, lawyers, and agents. With my head down, squeezing Liz's arm, I couldn't bear to look up, to make polite eye contact with the strangers around us, pretending to smile as if nothing were wrong. The elevator dropped as I stared at the floor falling out beneath me, diverting my mind; my eyes homed in on the shoes that encircled my feet. My gray boots stood close to Liz's blue flats, still standing taller than most. I couldn't distinguish the strangers around us, all in men's black leather shoes. My mind raced as they exited the elevator first, all I saw was white.

Liz held the heavy glass door open, letting me storm through unobstructed. Outside we walked in circles around the courtyard. "I'm sorry," she said, not surprised by my revelation, letting me absorb the information, realizing that unlike her, I hadn't thought of this earlier.

"I'm not rationalizing it…" she started, "just something to think about…" she paused, treading sensitively with her words. "Do you think they hire Muslims at the Israeli embassy?"

"But I'm not Israeli," I said.

"Maybe call Tyrone? " she shrugged. Needing to get back to her desk before anyone noticed, she left me with a tight hug.

I stood alone in the courtyard, waiting for Tyrone to pick up the phone. "Hey, what are you up to?" I asked.

"Working," he responded.

"Fatema just told me Jews can't work here," I blurted out.

"Yeah."

"Yeah?"

"I figured."

"Wha'do you mean?"

"I read the news."

"I read the news too," I said indignantly, even though he knew I didn't read the news. I looked to him, to calm me down, to talk me off the ledge.

Instead, he asked, "Any Black men in your office?"

The subtle reminder. Tyrone rarely spoke of his experience being the only Black man in the room, but when he did, I listened. In a classroom, a board room, a restaurant, a party, his experience shared by many and yet unacknowledged by the masses.

★ ★ ★

In Los Angeles, five months before the wedding, I sat alone on the bed in the rented room planning a seating chart at a table that I hoped would bring us closer together. The final list only included immediate family and our closest friends. There was no room for any guest who didn't believe in this union. A seat that was taken away from the table would go unnoticed by the guests, but the absence would fill the room. The uninvited shame would be there regardless, lingering in the corner. It was my beloved grandmother, who adored me and whom I adored, who would not fill her seat for the marriage she didn't believe in.

I was a shimmering star that lit up her eyes at every visit. With a kiss on the arm, she reminded me that I was "as sweet as brown shugah." Yet the woman born in 1916, who volunteered for over twenty years at an all-Black church in Memphis, Tennessee, hadn't seen life beyond the three right turns that she took to go left.

When my hand had gently brushed up against Tyrone's at the dinner table of my sister's wedding years prior, a quick click of her tongue had snapped to get my attention, shaking her head at me, signaling to immediately stop this unacceptable behavior. She couldn't say anything at that moment, but she didn't have to. Being polite kept her tongue tied, especially in front of Rabbi Bernstein, though even his approval wouldn't be enough for her to concede. A number of disapproving phone calls from my grandmother to my mother ensured we got the message.

Her absence would be covered by the stroke and dementia brought on weeks before the wedding, which protected her from not knowing that she was unable to attend the ceremony she wouldn't have celebrated. The unoccupied space would only briefly make it more comfortable for my mother and me, not having to deal with her disapproval of it all. But the guilt that I carried along with it was a heavier burden to bear, with the weight increasing as rapidly as her health declined.

It was hard for me to discern if my grandma's disapproval was because Tyrone was Black or not Jewish. It was easier for me not to know. I didn't want to rewrite her story by erasing the love she showed me my whole life. Instead, I would have to live with the regret of choosing not to challenge her, but I couldn't lie to myself. I loved my grandmother even though she was what some called "a little racist."

Chapter 13

Resources For Humans

"Did you hear the news?" Ashley asked, rushing into my office.

"What news?" I prodded, wanting her to confirm or deny what Fatema had said.

"The DC office got audited."

That wasn't the news I was looking for.

"Okay?"

"They owe hundreds of thousands of dollars."

"Who does?"

"Everyone who works there."

"What are you talking about?"

"The IRS is auditing embassy employees in DC, and we're next," she paused, "They noticed no one was paying their taxes. One of the staffers—been there for years—owes over three hundred thousand dollars."

I thought back to every time a handwritten check was left on my desk without any statement of deductions and I'd gleefully accepted it, taking the word of the office gossip as fact when I heard "foreign governments aren't taxed."

I called a family friend and trusted accountant, in New York, Jacob Goldberg. He gave me a discount on filing my taxes since I never had much to report.

"You kiddin' me?" he laughed, "Who are you listening to over there, anyway?" The paychecks seemed generous for someone working in education, but everything we dealt with was in such large amounts of money: the office suite near Beverly Hills, the student salaries, the chauffeur, the tuition payments.

"Ya know I don't hear much from my clients who didn't pay up." He paused. "They don't wanna waste their one call on me anymore." Clicking away at a calculator, Jacob said, "I estimate you only owe twelve thousand dollars at this point." There was silence over the line. I didn't need to do the math to add up my empty account. Instead, I calculated how long I'd have to work there to pay it off.

"How come I haven't gotten an invitation yet?" he asked. "You still marryin' the Black guy?"

★ ★ ★

The rule we all knew to abide by was broken. Office doors were shut, signaling an act of betrayal to Dr. Mohammad and a lockdown drill to everyone else. When I entered through the secured entrance to our suite, it didn't feel safe to be the only one in the corridor, but being confined in an office also seemed daunting. I tread carefully, arriving at my desk unde-tected, sitting in silence, facing my computer, staring at the unlit screen, not making any movement beyond peering out the corner of my eyes. Out the window, the ground appeared miles away, with flashes of color from the cars zig-zagging far below, while inside, our office space was motionless.

Without turning my head, I could identify every person who walked by, distinguishing the sound of every cough, the scent of each coworker's perfume. Anytime someone left discreetly through the back door, it was in my line of sight. With so few employees, a stranger would stand out as soon as they managed to access our fortress.

Two men in dark suits headed in my direction, their faces indistinguishable. Viraj stood between them. I stared at the ground, slightly hunched over, fiddling to reach the computer's power button beneath the desk. A metallic taste filled my mouth, readying my body to vomit in the trashcan next to the tower running the PC.

The three men were heading for the backdoor. Two empty cubicles that awaited future staff created an aisle for Viraj to walk down, the two men linked on either side of his arms. His steps were slow with intention, a stride shorter than usual, as if dragging a ball and chain. His shoulders were pulled back so tight, forcing him to hold his head up. Enormous sweat marks underneath his armpits drenched his button-down shirt. The business jacket he started wearing more often hung awkwardly over his wrists, joined together behind him, and when it slipped slightly, metal handcuffs shined through, restraining him less than the men on either side.

Thirty minutes later, office doors opened, but not a word was spoken. Liz and I were always the last to hear of any office rumblings. Ashely's voice ruminated in my head: "We don't abide my American labor laws." I would need to remember to Google that on my personal computer at home.

Chapter 14

All Choked Up

*E*ntering Dr. Mohammad's office, I heard a desk drawer slam shut, catching him frazzled and off guard. Popping a candy into his mouth, he looked like a child not wanting his parent to see. He never ate at his desk like the rest of us. He sat there day and night, not ever leaving to eat or take a break or use the employee restroom. His robust frame that reflected his stance on office practices now looked a little broken. His face pale white was losing color in an unnatural manner.

"Are you choking?" I asked hurriedly. "Nod if you're choking." I wrung my hands around my neck and stuck my tongue out, showing what I believed translated into the international sign for choking. Dr. Mohammad was definitely choking. I stared directly at him, cueing him to respond with even just a blink of an eye, as that was all the time we had. "Dr. Mohammad, I am trained in CPR and the mouth-to-mouth thing," I said in a hushed voice, knowing not to draw any unwanted attention from the staff outside his office. I knew he could not be touched by the female staff, but I wasn't sure if there were exceptions in the case of an emergency. I did know that waiting was not an option.

I now knew how to read him. I understood what he needed, and the look of shock on his face no longer startled me as it once did. "Are you choking?" I repeated, pausing to mouth slowly, having him focus on my lips, "I. Can. Help. You."

I jumped up to take action, to do whatever I needed to do—grab him from behind, arms wrapped around his body, touch him below his chest, thrust him back onto my small frame, lean him over his chair, use the weight of his own body against mine until I could hear the relief come from his mouth, knocking the wind and anything lodged out of him.

My action was louder than any words. But ultimately, just seeing me jump out of my seat was enough of an impact to give him the jolt he needed, dislodging the candy from his throat, leaving him sweaty, red in the face, and breathing heavily.

"I'll come back later," I said, allowing him to compose himself, leaving before he had a chance to get choked up on his words.

Moments later, back at my desk, there was a box with a neatly tied bow and a card. A gift from Dr. Saamia for my wedding was anything but predictable. I pulled out a shiny pair of red leather racing gloves. *Thank you?* I thought, picturing myself with the tight leather covering my white knuckles as I shifted gears from neutral to first, sitting in bumper-to-bumper traffic on Sunset Boulevard in my brown Honda.

"Go. Go. Go," Hala came waving her arm to get me up.

"Go where?" I asked.

"You have to go now," she exclaimed. "To the doctor's office, she is waiting for you."

Unfamiliar with the customs in giving and receiving gifts from a high-ranking Kuwaiti female, I quickly learned that the protocol was to sprint down the hall, hurrying to immediately thank her for the racing gloves that she could not hand to me herself.

"Go already," Hala snapped.

I sprang to my feet, knowing I would have to tread lightly. Dr. Mohammad's line of vision looked straight shot down the corridor to Dr. Saamia's office, and I was not interested in a game of tit for tat if he caught me speaking with his rival.

On my tippy toes, I pretended to be walking down to talk to Abdul Baatin, facing him to say hello; I stepped into Dr. Saamia's office backward, not yet facing her, spinning around on my heels to blurt out, "Thank you."

Fatema and Dr. Saamia looked as surprised by my outburst as I was to find them together, whispering. I hesitated, standing in the door frame, my feet grounded in the hallway outside her office, my head peeked in, my eyes glancing over my shoulder. Dr. Saamia locked her eyes to mine, keeping my attention on her. "Thank you," I repeated. Her grin acknowledged that my gratitude was received. "The gloves will look great..." I paused, wondering where I would wear the dramatic bright red leather accessory in eighty-five degree weather in LA. "The gloves will look great on a night out. Thank you," I said in a hushed voice, with an excited tone. "I'm sorry to interrupt," I used as my excuse to leave her office, tiptoeing backward.

"Hey," Holly said, grabbing me by my arm, pulling me into the kitchen. "We should go to jail." The only trace of Viraj's was a half-empty bowl of chocolates and the porn found on his computer.

Oh God. I stopped in my tracks.

"To see Viraj," she continued.

Oh God. Fearing who might overhear the conversation, passing by, I took a step backwards into the doorframe, both feet outside of the kitchen. I knew where I stood.

"He's all alone. We should take him some food."

Unfamiliar with prison practices, I couldn't imagine they were reformed enough to allow snacks. I shook my head no without saying a word and tiptoed backward, heading as far away from the conversation as possible.

Arriving back to my seat, I let out a sigh of relief sitting back in my chair. "I thought you might need these," Liz said, holding up a ziplock bag filled with homemade chocolate fudge. She opened my desk drawer and slipped them in.

"What are those?" Nahla asked, interrupting my racing thoughts as I slammed the drawer shut, uninterested in sharing anything Liz baked with someone so undeserving. She wasn't looking at the snack. Her eyes focused on the gift box left out on my desk.

"They're racing gloves." I said, "Wedding gift from Dr. Saamia."

"Did Dr. Mohammad get you anything?" she asked in her typical pot-stirring manner.

I looked at Liz. She knew. Dr. Mohammad gave me a gift I couldn't show Nahla. He gave me an opportunity. A job in my field that I needed and wanted desperately. He threw me a lifesaver when I needed it, and even though I was still treading water, he believed I could swim.

My pause was too long to keep Nahla interested. She left the room after pointing out that there was no big box tied with a fancy bow. It didn't matter to her. But it mattered to me.

I heard my name shouted from down the hall. "Jessica Keith," Dr. Mohammad called out. Though the sound of choking is silent, I rushed to save him.

"I need your help," he said, sounding out of breath. Looking over his body, I tried to assess the situation quickly. "Promise me you won't leave me."

"I'm right here, Dr. Mohammad. I'm not going any-where," I reassured him.

"Promise me you won't leave me..."

"Of course," I replied, unsure of what we were talking about.

"The ministry..." he started rambling, "There was a crime... Viraj...money laundered... Dr. Saamia will blame me.... The ministry will blame me. They will shut us down laughing," his voice trembled. "He was not who I thought he was. Promise me you won't leave, not now. We aren't stable enough."

"I promise." With two months until my wedding, I looked towards Dr. Mohammad, and said, "I do."

Chapter 15

The Weight Before The Wedding

"Her hips are perfect for childbearing," Nubia said to Hala as they stood in line to use the copying machine. I turned around, curious to know who they were talking about. The two women were pointing at my backside, eyebrows raised. Nubia motioned what appeared to be squeezing watermelons. "So juicy."

"Sweet for the big day," Hala said.

"Mashallah," Nubia said, patting herself on the back. "We've helped, no?" she asked me, eyebrows raised, eager for my reply.

I stared back. Shaking my head. Puzzled by the conversation.

"Hidden treasures in your chest," Hala chimed in. "You liked?"

Engulfed by so many secrets, I stood with my photocopies in hand, lost in translation. Believing her two words would explain it all, Hala blurted out, "Chocolate swirls."

"Don't forget the white chocolate cranberry bars." Nubia held her hand up to get credit for her baked goods. "In your desk drawer."

All the homemade treats. I hadn't shared a crumb, eating every last bite. I assumed Liz made them all, not even thinking twice about putting them in my mouth.

"Thank you?"

"They have worked," Hala said, giving Nubia a congratulatory, swift pat on the butt. "You look," she paused, nodding her head in approval, "so big. From behind."

And there it was, the help they thought I needed. Unlike Americans "shedding for the wedding," my Arab colleagues described a full-figured bride like a piece of fruit. She would appear sweet if she was bountiful and not as tasty if she was overripe and too plump. My indulgences never weighed on me, but I did want to look tasty when I said, "I do."

"They are trying to plump me up," I IM'd Liz.

She knew what the women were up to, replying, "They just want your peaches to be tasty."

I grinned at the words on the screen like a love note popping up. It reminded me of Tyrone when we had met at work in the Fall of 2000 in San Diego. "Sorry can't come by cubicle today," he emailed from his office one floor above. "You're too distracting—in the good kind of way."

Hoping to catch his eye, I dressed in my typical uniform—a Lycra dress stretched around my curves paired with knee high black boots with a thick heel to balance my short frame.

My hard work was paying off. Trying to get his attention was much more fun than keeping his interest. My stomach couldn't digest the dumps of adrenaline that had me gagging on bile once he asked me out.

An email popped up. "I think I'm coming down with something," Tyrone's message read. "Do you wanna take a sick day on Friday, maybe go to the beach?"

I stared at the email until I could read it with my eyes closed. Then I powered off my computer, pretending I never saw it.

When I didn't reply, he texted, "Want a nibble? I know a great place."

I could hear his voice, so friendly and upbeat, come through in the message with just eight words. I imagined the perfect reply, but it was too late. My fingers had a mind of their own hitting send after typing, "I just ate."

Surely, he wouldn't ask me out again—definitely not if he could read my thoughts and the dead end that they were leading me to.

Don't fuck this up. Tyrone was a dream, but at twenty-three years old, my thoughts flooded with nightmares of "what-if's." *Don't fuck this up.* I racked my brain to convince myself I could do this. I would just need fresh air, lots of space, somewhere not too crowded, with no lines, no smell of food, nowhere dark, and for us to drive separately.

I sent Tyrone a follow up text, "Frisbee golf?"

★ ★ ★

"Done," I announced from the dressing room of the bridal store to my friend Leah, waiting on an ivory tufted bench. Behind her on the wall, a sign with gold cursive on a blank canvas framed the words, "No longer a bridesmaid." She drove up to LA to save the day yet again. First driving me to the interview and now helping me find a wedding dress. She scheduled an appointment at the only dress shop reserving a one-hour time slot available for a bride whose wedding was eight weeks away.

"I'm not trying on another dress," I said, arms crossed, coming out of the dressing room, wearing my flip flops, jeans, and a T-shirt. After three sample sizes didn't fit, I decided not to wiggle my way in and out of one more heavy white dress with scratchy tule. The attendant pulled enough dresses out for me to see that I looked like a bowl of marshmallows, white puffs everywhere. Knowing she stood within earshot, I attempted to squeeze myself in, sweating on the fabric, hoping she didn't hear the seam rip.

"Are you all done here?" the bridal attendant asked, looking at her watch. The moment she asked, "What type of dress are you looking for?" and I responded with, "Just something off the rack," the bridal attendant no longer had time to help.

Leah looked at the woman, then me—we were both done. "We still have forty-five minutes," she spoke up, knowing I had no interest in playing Cinderella while every clock was ticking.

"You might want to check the department stores," the woman suggested, hoping that would be the sendoff of an ill-prepared bride.

Leah looked at me and then at the attendant, we were in a standoff, both of us with our arms crossed. "I'll try 'em on for you," Leah said, jumping to her feet.

The woman's face lit up with hope, rushing to grab a new batch of dresses.

"This one will look great on you," the attendant said, looking at Leah's perfectly tanned surfer body. It only took Leah a brief moment to slip into the off-white silk dress that clung to her body, highlighting all the right curves. There was no ring on her finger. Although she was single, hers was already picked out. Her figure was a skinnier version of mine, her dark hair longer and shinier. If I wore four-inch heels, I would almost be her height on flat feet. She spun around on her tippy toes, admiring her reflection in each mirror. She looked like a model in a catalog, running through wildflowers to get to her man who waited his whole life for her.

"Done. I'll just take that one," I said, my voice interrupting the moment.

"You'll need the larger size," the attendant said, her gaze still admiring Leah.

"I'll take that one," I repeated, believing neither the dress nor the size mattered.

The attendant scoffed, "It's just like diamonds and husbands. Yah can't return 'em."

★ ★ ★

"Is the office putting us on a diet?" I instant messaged Liz.

"You have ample time outside office hours to consume food and beverages," a memo stated on August 10th, 2009. It was left on every desk in our office, welcoming the staff as we arrived at work. "Consuming any food or drink is prohibited within the office, including running the coffee pots. No one is authorized to take a lunch break."

"What's the deal with this?" I asked Ashley, holding up the memo I knew she prepared on behalf of Dr. Mohammad.

"It's Ramadan."

"And?"

"And no breaks allowed."

"How is that possible?"

"We don't abide by American labor laws," she said, as her answer to everything. "Get this. Office hours, ten to three for…the whole month."

I felt like a child playing dress-up told, "No more snacks."

"Ramadon't bother calling me after 3 p.m.," Ashley cackled.

The front doors of our suite separated the Angelenos who found devilish ways to stay slim and the Muslims who fasted to feel closer to God. Since Ramadan began and the five devout Muslims in the office began fasting, the clock in our office began ticking slower than ever. No food. No drink. No perfume or scent of any kind could linger off the body, as it was considered too distracting and disruptive to the senses.

"Seriously?" Nahla scoffed, rolling her eyes at me, staring at my stomach. 10:45 a.m., day two of Ramadan, my stomach was growling loud enough for Nahla to hear over the copy machine, drawing unwanted attention to my body.

Back at my desk, I IM'd Liz, "This is why I don't diet." Missing a meal felt like being on an intermittent fasting plan. "It's all too LA for me."

"Totally," she replied.

"Ready for secret mission?" I asked.

"Leaving now," she wrote as the cue to leave our desks, exit different doors, and meet in the elevator at the same time to avoid bringing any attention to our covert plan. Our office was like a rollercoaster ride, exciting and daunting, with twists and turns we never expected. Liz was always next to me for the ride. She knew I was just hoping to survive, and I knew she was hoping there wasn't a line. Together, we hopped on the elevator. The keeper of so many of our secrets was in the death trap.

"You heard about Holly, right?" I asked.

"She hit that nail on her own coffin," Liz whispered.

Holly didn't make it to the end of her three-month trial. Her plan to bust Viraj out of jail, coming to his defense, never left my lips. The rumor mill spilled out that she made a few too many errors wiring money to the wrong accounts, sealing her fate. Unlike Viraj, there was no escort out. She just wasn't invited to come back ever again.

I squeezed Liz's hand, holding my breath as we dropped down nineteen stories to the basement of the building. Navigating through the dimly lit hall, we passed by the one-hour dry cleaners, a post office, and a shoe shine, arriving at our final destination: the Starbucks.

"Ramadan Kareem," Liz cheered to a shot of espresso with a splash of milk. Without saying a word, I clinked my paper cup to hers. Drinking the shot of espresso in one giant swig, I didn't take the moment all in, unaware of our words and actions being so similar to gentiles who shout out "Happy Yom Kippur" to Jews on the saddest day of our year, sounding like they're cheering at a funeral.

Back in the elevator, Liz pulled out a tin, the same size of the container that I slipped into my bra every morning to carry my in-case-of-emergency benzodiazepines. We both knew we couldn't bring back any evidence. Neither coffee nor eau de café was on the approved list for the month. Liz's sleek case held tiny mints in her back pocket. I took one and, using my tongue like a windshield wiper, I swooshed it back and forth across my mouth, hoping to get rid of the smell.

"A little time to work out is one thing," I joked to Liz. "But this is not a diet I had in mind."

★　★　★

Away from Rodeo Drive and Sunset Boulevard, closer to Nordstrom Rack and TJ Maxx, I found a gym along my commute that was more my style. In a Jewish pocket of LA between a delicatessen, Joan's on Third, and The Original Farmer's Market, I found Swerve, a gym and dance studio where I only saw women exercising. When I read on the website "At Swerve, you are welcome to be just who you are," I saw it as a sign.

I wore spandex booty shorts and a tank top that barely covered my sports bra in a class where no one flaunted their bits. Most women came to class heads covered with a scarf, long sleeve shirts, and leggings worn underneath ankle length skirts. With an Orthodox shul down the street, the women were within walking distance to the temple and to dance class where they could sing along to Madonna's "Like a Prayer."

The teachers at Swerve were the stars behind the stars, boasting highbrow bios including choreographing Lionel Richie's "Dancing on a Ceiling," yet pretension never entered the door. Women gathered in the discreetly located studio where together they could move their bodies in a space that wasn't on display. The music was world beats, which included the Beastie Boys and Jewish singers like Matisyahu. No one cared to notice the only man in the room, drumming on a djembe, keeping the beat for a dance battle where everyone felt like they were winning.

It was during Ramadan that I stopped wandering and found a place I fit in. While my Muslim colleagues were fasting from sunrise to sunset, I was surrounded by Hebrews, dancing the grapevine to A Tribe Called Quest rapping "Ham 'N' Eggs."

★ ★ ★

"Happy day of reckoning" wouldn't work as a greeting for Yom Kippur, so I steered away from joking "have a quick-fast." Instead, I grinned at Dr. Mohammad the second week of Ramadan just before leaving the office at 3 p.m. on Friday. "May you have a meaningful fast," I said.

Getting off two hours early on a Friday felt like reason enough to celebrate. "I'm coming to you this time," I said to Tyrone over the phone with plans to commute to San Diego, giving Tyrone a break and myself a challenge. I left the office right on time, which was two hours early, skipping over a few blocks of rush hour, arriving downtown at Union Station by four, parking below, its own hidden gem, a steal at only seven dollars a night. To celebrate the successful drive without a sedative, I popped a pill for the train ride, letting it take over my body, with plenty of time to let it set into cruise control. With a little less than an hour, I spent the time finalizing seating charts and menus before the 5 p.m. train pulled up. Pleased to find an empty seat on the packed train, I pulled the drawstrings on the hood of my sweatshirt, creating blinders from the swarming crowds around me, packed with commuters, for the busiest ride of the week. Zipping up the front, I felt the comfort of a hug wrapped around my body as I stretched my legs out, slouching lower in my seat to reach the footrest as I chilled out, giving in to the sedative.

Neatly wrapped engagement gifts sat outside under the porch swing by the front door of the two-bedroom craftsman house Tyrone rented near Balboa Park in San Diego. He was living in it alone during the week, leaving it empty on the weekends to stay with me in LA. To afford back-paying the taxes, I gave my roommate notice and moved again into a studio apartment. Forced to sign a year lease with a longer commute, I was moving farther away from living happily ever after.

"They're here," I said to Tyrone, smiling from ear to ear, holding the box of wedding invitations in my hands. They were mailed to Tyrone as my address had changed four times in the last three months. I unwrapped the package carefully, unfolding the tissue paper that protected the heavy cardstock. In gold print, a Hebrew quote was pressed into the thick paper for our guests to read: "All my love every day, every day with my love."

Tyrone pulled out the invitations to see the envelopes on the bottom of the box. He looked at the address on the RSVP cards. Replies would be sent to the house he rented for us to live in, but the writing was on the wall when I signed the year lease. He knew I wouldn't be living in the house with him. We weren't married yet, and Tyrone was already doing the math for the taxes we would soon be filing together. Renting two homes, now back-paying taxes, and throwing a wedding—during a recession. With our delicate wedding invitation in the palm of his hand, he looked deep into my eyes and said, "I'm gonna have to get a roommate."

★   ★   ★

The weekend was over before either of us settled in comfortably. With my bagged dinner in tow, Tyrone dropped me off at the train station for my commute back to LA. We were headed in two different directions. While he cruised to his happy hour, I jumped on the train, hoping to get a window seat alone where I could look out into the darkness, dreaming of being asleep on my futon.

Tyrone and I weren't concerned with what the light at the end of the tunnel looked like. Our wants were simple. Tyrone didn't want the train to be late. I wanted to remember if it was a street sweeping day, not wanting to pay the price of a ticket or worse, not having anywhere to park the car once I returned from the train station, leaving me to drive around in circles counting down the minutes left to sleep. Before this job, Tyrone had shouldered the weight of carrying the financial burden for too long. The temp work had been unfulfilling, and because the hours ran into the evening, it often kept me from seeing him. Now, I made enough for rent in another city and a train ticket headed away from my fairy tale ending.

After the train pulled up to my stop at 11 p.m., I walked briskly through the dimly lit underground parking lot, beneath the train station, with my backpack strapped onto my shoulders as I rethought the deal on parking, deciding it wasn't worth my life. I held my car fob in one hand with my thumb ready to hit the emergency alarm button. On the twenty-five minute drive back to the studio, I lost sleep over how long it would take me to find a parking space on the metered street within a reasonable walking proximity. Circling the neighborhood where I knew no one, I now hoped to survive running in the darkness, towards my home, where no one would notice if I went missing.

★   ★   ★

"Never look when your wife is giving birth or later you will never want to look at your wife," Dr. Mohammad said, sitting in his office, laughing along with a rosy-cheeked new hire Nickolas. Dr. Mohammad found plenty of time to bond with the conservative Mormon who came from a large family. Meanwhile, the ladies considered it a bold move—bringing in a male advisor the third week of Ramadan, using shorter days to ease him in. But there was no time to gossip about it. While the women rushed around to finish an eight-hour day in five hours, Nick looked comfortable sitting across from Dr. Mohammad, kicking back in the leather chair where none of the ladies ever rested their laurels.

"My friends call me 'St. Nick,' but you can just call me 'Nick,'" he laughed, introducing himself, putting his hand out to shake mine as Dr. Mohammad's watchful eye pretended not to notice.

Showing Dr. Mohammad where I stood, I cupped my hands behind my back, showing my respect by not touching another male during Ramadan in front of Dr. Mohammad. While he couldn't look directly at me, I knew Dr. Mohammad was watching.

"Ramadan Mubarak," I grinned towards Dr. Mohammad before heading out for my Friday commute down to San Diego.

"Inshallah," Dr. Mohammad replied.

"Click," the Polaroid sounded as a photo developed out of the front of the camera. While a picture couldn't capture all the love I had for Tyrone, we snapped photos of the two of us embracing with giant grins across our faces as we laughed, holding signs for the wedding, revealing a snapshot of the life we wanted.

We planned for our guests to all sit together at a single long table. We would join together as one with seats marked by name cards, the Polaroid pictures of Tyrone and me, with our guests' names below in Sharpie. In lieu of table numbers, the palm of our hands held out a sign that read a value significant for our marriage in the photo. Arranged along the entirety of the table, noting the area where our friends and family could find their place to celebrate, words colored in with magic markers would mark where they fit in. The values, "kindness, gratitude, unity, love, laughter, mindfulness, friendship, happiness, growth, compassion, and commitment," would highlight what was most important to Tyrone and me. The words would be placed in heavy glass frames reflecting the transparency of our relationship.

To get a glimpse into the life I could be living, I stayed in San Diego Sunday night so that I wouldn't miss happy hour with our friends. For the last week of Ramadan, I would be testing my stamina catching the train Monday morning, feeling like I was making a deal with the devil. In exchange for the extra time on Sunday, I would lose sleep Monday. With a 5:15 a.m. wake up, I could be on the train by 5:45 a.m. for the 6 a.m. departure from San Diego that would pull into Los Angeles Union Station at 9 a.m. Driving from downtown to Century City, a reverse commute, would only take an hour, allowing me to arrive in time for work at 10 a.m. For seven extra dollars, I could leave the parking lot in broad daylight. It only cost me five hours of sleep and four hours commuting.

Unable to fight the sedative on only a few hours of sleep, I passed out in my window seat, setting the alarm to make sure I woke up in time to get dressed for work in the bathroom of the train, splashing the water on my face, keeping my lips tight to avoid consuming any of the liquid that came out below the hazard sign that read "Non-potable. Do not drink." I tried to see my reflection through the clouded mirror. In my hazy, sleep-deprived, sedated state, I wondered if this was all worth it.

Chapter 16

Fasting Forwards

"So delicious on the tongue," Dr. Saamia said as her arms reached out to me with her offerings. A new day, and Ramadan was over. "A dance in the mouth," she said, holding out a bag of candy corn. I reached my hand in and grabbed some. I ran into her in the kitchen tasting the Halloween candies the first week of October, two and a half weeks before the wedding.

"Such a sight," she grinned. "Look at all of this," she said, opening the cupboard to reveal bags of candy she bought and stored in the office for trick-or-treating at the end of the month. "Everything here is just so good," she said, showing off the assortment.

Through the transparent wrapping, the candies were a tempting view. But I couldn't even take a step closer. Spotting a red vine in the variety bag was all it took. The memory of my teenage self came rushing back, as it always did. Even wrapped, the scent of the candy I associated with vulnerability was too strong.

On a date with my neighbor, Christian, a blue-eyed senior at an all-boys Catholic school, we sat at the bottom of the University of New Mexico's basketball stadium, the PIT, built thirty-seven feet below ground. He pretended that we were meeting his parents, convincing security to let us go all the way down to the floor seats. I was the new girl in town, unfamiliar with my surroundings. In the land of enchantment, I found myself in desolation without breathing space to think about how I ended up in this hole.

Trying to blend in by keeping casual, I wore hiking boots and a weathered navy blue sweatshirt. But I immediately stood out as the only one not representing the home team in red and black. Even though I felt invisible, everyone could see I wasn't from there. I took off the sweatshirt and tied it around my waist, hoping to blend into the background, seeming neutral in my all-white turtleneck.

I knew my new neighbor Christian was trouble, but I was excited by it. He was good looking, and I liked that he gave me attention, even though I knew he gave it to all the girls. If I were familiar with my surroundings, I might have had the confidence to know this game wasn't where I wanted to be. When my stomach churned, I assumed it was butterflies—I didn't know it was my gut telling me, "get out."

"You want some?" Christian asked. Hearing a crinkling sound as he ripped open the package of red vines, I nodded, unable to use my voice. November 1994, unlike the cool girls at school who were fluent in all things boy, I was a young seventeen-year-old—unable to translate my own body language. When he offered me one, I couldn't say no. The licorice on my tongue felt like I was chewing on the twisted wax of a candle. I forced it to the back of my throat and tried to swallow it like taking a pill without water. The licorice clawed at my dry throat, triggering it to close up. "Hold on," I said in a whisper, trying not to open my mouth, surprised the words escaped.

Needing to find air, I jumped out of my seat and turned to race up the stairs, trying to escape the rising heat in my body. The fans were swarming around me, rushing to take their seats before the game started, while I was like a salmon swimming upstream in a river during a drought, gasping for a breath. The crowd cheering to the marching band booming sounded like a whisper in the background as the screaming in my head pierced my eardrums.

I ran with all my strength, up the hundreds of steps, but I was shouldering the weight of my nerves like cinder blocks bound to my body. It was so steep, and the altitude put an additional level of stress on my lungs I still wasn't used to. I was so close to the edge, but I didn't know, as my eyes were focused down on the ground. That one last breath I took wouldn't get me to the top. I couldn't hold it in.

In my last gasp for air, I threw up the red vine all over my white turtleneck. I raced up every step of the way but lost it all trying to get out. I stood hunched over, shaking with exhaustion, surrounded by the crowds of spectators without anyone noticing me. The loneliness felt like a fire burning in my body while the silence was an oppressive, unendurable weight—but I couldn't find my voice; it was muted by the feeling that my parents diminished. I could have felt brave that night, having shown resilience, but instead, I felt hurried to cover up the shame.

A pink color stained my white turtleneck, which was now see-through, with brown particles stuck to it, as I frantically tried to wipe off the evidence in the bathroom with a wet paper towel that only disintegrated onto my shirt the harder I rubbed. *I can't manage.* My illogical self decided that my only option was to put the sweatshirt back on over the turtleneck, hiding what happened. Going back down the flights of stairs, I covered my wounds, so the cheering fans wouldn't smell my fear, as I walked back into the pit of the colosseum.

"Don't you worry, *Habibti*," Hala said, breaking my thought, finding me standing alone in the kitchen with an uncertain look on my face, the candy corn stuck to my skin as orange dripped down the palm of my hand. With a wet paper towel, Hala started wiping them off into the trash. "I'll help," she said. When there were no longer any treats in my hand, she looked up at me and said, "For after your wedding." She added, "I'll let you know if you are getting too fat."

I recounted the story to Liz in the hallway while waiting for the elevator. At lunchtime, the doors to the elevator opened in time for Liz and me to hear a woman inside exclaim, "My nipples were nearly ripped off." We attempted to step inside discreetly, but then Liz hit the close door button a few too many times. The two other women leaned up against the back wall of the elevator with stylish messy buns, dressed in business chic straight skirts and blazers. One of them stood out more than the other. Underneath her dark blazer and wrinkled white blouse, a dried liquid around her breast peeked out. She pulled at her blazer, trying to cover the stain and an elastic line circling above her loose belly. Her ensemble revealed the look she likely wasn't going for: postpartum in maternity clothes.

"So then he cackles…" the woman continued, "she's jerking off again."

"They're such dicks," her friend responded.

"He jiggles the locked door handle. Every. Time."

The woman's arms wrapped around her body, cradling under her bra for support. She recounted ripping off her breast pump upon hearing her male coworker pretending to enter her locked office door marked with the sign, "Do not disturb."

Exiting the elevator, I wondered when Dina planned to tell Dr. Mohammad so we could all celebrate. Liz and I walked through the lobby without batting an eyelash, walking straight outside through the heavy glass doors. Just beyond the exit, by the well-manicured bushes, Abdul Baatin and Dr. Mohammad's chauffeur were hunkered down smoking. We grinned but let them be, as always, so they could smoke their cigarettes in peace, without being disturbed.

Sitting at the bistro table, I recounted the story of the basketball game vomit-apocalypse. "Worst date ever," Liz replied, feeling my pain.

"Hardly," I said. "Did I ever tell you about my first homecoming date?" I was fifteen years old, dressed in an off the shoulder red mini dress with sleeves that puffed up to my ears and a big red bow across my chest. My mother lent me her black velvet clutch. "His dad dropped us off at Benihanas for dinner." The smell off the grill wafted to where the hostess stood guarding a bowl of wrapped fortune cookies. Over her shoulder, I could see the chefs in their tall white hats juggling their kitchen tools, flipping their knives as they spun around to captivate their audience hungry for a show. The oil sizzled hitting the hot grill, popping off, sounding like a firecracker.

The chef threw a handful of unkosher raw shrimp on the grill, spun around and then tossed them in the air with his spatula. "I only had enough time to say, 'I'll be right back,' step fifteen feet away, open my mom's clutch, and throw up in it." It filled her bag and covered my shoes.

"Oh. My. God. What did your parents say?"

"My mom said I couldn't borrow her purses anymore."

"What about your dad?"

"He cleaned my shoes."

"I mean were they worried about your nerves?"

"Not really."

"Isn't your dad a psychiatrist?" she asked.

"Yep, but you know the saying about a shoemaker's child?"

"Sure do. Remember my dad's a professor? First thing we learned was don't bother asking him."

★ ★ ★

Mohammad, a student on scholarship, stood in the doorframe, knocking on the wall outside my office. He smiled, showing off a babyface and a mouth filled with braces. I assumed from the skinny frame he hadn't learned to hit up Taco Bell like the other males who didn't know how to cook yet. "I need my form signed," he said in lieu of "Hello."

"That's what I'm here for," I replied.

Emails and phone calls from the male students flooded my systems, drowning me in work. The students so rarely came into the office. Face-to-face interaction was a breath of fresh air, hearing what the outside world looked like from a student's perspective.

Yet the only sound was of Mohammad putting the paper down on my desk to sign.

I saw the dotted line but held him captive for a moment, pausing to sign off on the form, to check in on what his reality looked like.

"How ya doin'?" I asked. "A lot of change, right?" I was eager to hear in person what isn't relayed over the phone.

Mohammad nodded, not saying a word.

"I've been there," I said, knowing too well the way my body ached, feeling like an outsider at a new school. "I still remember." I kept pausing, hoping Mohammad would chime in.

"It almost hurts my stomach to think about it," I said.

His eyebrows darted in, cueing me to clarify. "I was just so nervous," I explained. "Everything felt off."

He broke his silence. "You were sick?"

"No. No," I said, realizing my attempt to connect was leading us astray. "All the nerves...I just...it was so hard...I didn't feel good." Stopping myself before the acid started to tear up my stomach as a reminder that the pain was still there. I signed on the dotted line and pushed the paper to Mohammad, who took it into his hand. His face looked relieved.

"I have lost sixteen pounds," he mumbled, looking down at the paper.

"I'm sorry?" I replied.

"Throwing up," he said. "Friends told me to ask a girl out."

"What?" I asked, not needing him to explain another word.

He looked down. Questioning if he said too much.

"No… No, I'm sorry." I said, looking towards his eyes. "Me too." In a hushed voice, I whispered to him. "I just get so nervous," I said. "No one ever gets it."

With the relief of not having to say it out loud, one glance at each other shared the anxiety unrecognizable to others.

I wanted to bring him close to me, smothering him in a hug, wrapping my covered arms around him, squeezing him tightly while whispering in his ear, "You're not alone."

Instead, I threw my arms around my own body, to hug myself, saying out loud, "This is for you," showing Mohammad the hug was intended for him.

"Can you help?"

"That's what I'm here for," I said, knowing how to navigate his university's safety net with counseling services. One phone call could have him on a waiting list for months, minimalizing the pain, deterring him from ever going. But this was a system I knew how to work, getting him seen that same day.

When he looked at me, he knew we came from two different worlds. Nothing about us appeared the same. Yet, I knew what he meant when he said, "You are my sister."

★ ★ ★

"Kuwait doesn't have the Flintstones" was in a curly font on one side of Dr. Saamia's mug. On the other side, it said, "but Abu Dabi do."

"You like?" Dr. Saamia asked when I stopped to get some water in the kitchen at work. I smiled at her mug as she was pouring a cup of tea. "My new shoes?" she asked, redirecting my glance.

I looked down and couldn't see anything beneath her head to toe covering. A gold-colored scarf was wrapped around her head, outlining her face with sequins adorned on the trim. A floor-length leopard print dress covered her arms and legs but unbuttoned to the bottom of her cleavage, which would unveil her figure, except she wore a beige-colored turtleneck underneath. From beneath her dress, she stuck her toe out, revealing clunky black sneakers. "Oh," I said in an enthusiastic tone, covering up my unenthusiasm.

"They shape your butt," she said, bringing my attention to the conversation. "They are this new invention. Get you in shape as you walk," she said in a hushed voice, about to share her secret. "They're called Skechers."

Detailing her new exercise regime, she noted her strolls at lunchtime around the courtyard wearing her Skechers Shape-Ups advertised to lift your butt simply by wearing and walking.

With no way to gauge her results, I noticed Dr. Saamia gradually started making small changes to her diet, no longer taking three-hour lunches to eat out in Beverly Hills while the staff sat outside rushing to eat their brown-bagged lunches. Instead, she started bringing in home-made food made by her in-home staff.

Looking up and down my post-Ramadan figure, she asked, "How do *you* exercise?"

"I have a place I go," I said. "Come."

My heart stopped the moment the words left my tongue. The typical reply would translate as sincere. Dr. Mohammad would be furious if he found out we were meeting up, behind his back. Was there any way she could accept the informal invitation from an American staffer?

"*Shukran, shukran,*" Dr. Saamia said graciously.

Did she just say thank you or no thank you? I wondered. *What would she even wear to a gym?*

I noticed several Orthodox Jewish women in ankle-length skirts with scarfs used to cover their heads or secure their wigs, as they arrived in the most unconventional manner for LA. I assumed it was unorthodox for these women to drive, seeing them come on foot.

"I try to make the 5:30 class," I said to Dr. Saamia, slowing down my words to elongate, "Yoga Booty Baaaaaallett," oddly changing my intonation to ensure she would not be able to translate this into a booty-shaking class. The more I went on in detail, the more I realized there was no way she could go. A devout Muslim woman, a foreign diplomat, would not be caught shaking her butt with an American employee. I wondered how many rules she would break in the Orthodox neighborhood of West Hollywood, the gay mecca of LA. Brushing shoulders against the men passing by on the sidewalk dressed in mesh tops and running shorts heading out for "cock-tail hour." Without a valet, there was no place for her Mercedes, shipped from abroad. The license plate "KUWAIT1" competed for attention with the diplomatic designation.

That evening I arrived at the 5:30 yoga booty ballet class in my daisy duke spandex shorts and a tank top that ironically shouted in bold letters, "no fear, no reward."

The studio felt like a club where I could dance at night without the hassle of staying up till 10 p.m. for it to open. The warmup started with pulsing in first position to Eurythmics' "Would I Lie to You?" A live drummer off to the side beat a bongo while the instructor shouted, "Grapevine to the right.

In four, three, two..." Like we were dancing the hora, we grapevined to the left and right a few times while fist-pumping to warm up our arms.

The music was loud enough to blast out the sounds from my work day, giving my mind a break, allowing my body a turn at exhausting itself. There were so many places to be judged, but here I didn't have to watch my step. I was free to move without actually having any rhythm. "Squat, ladies," the teacher yelled, "squeeze those cheeks. Show me you want it!" She shouted, thrusting on her squat.

Singing along to Madonna's "Like a Virgin," the mirrored wall reflected the women thrusting in sync. The Orthodox women stayed in the back corner, dancing as the instructor shouted, "Get it, ladies." It was hard to see their faces, but I could hear giggling coming from the back row. "How bad do you want it?" the teacher shouted. *How awkward if she came*, I reiterated to myself, noticing a woman dancing in the back was wearing the same Sketchers as Dr. Saamia's. I squinted at the mirror to see the Orthodox women squatting down, revealing Dr. Saamia. I knew immediately I would pay for it later. We both would.

Chapter 17

Do Not Stop To Smell The Roses

I pictured Dr. Mohammad at the wedding, being ushered to take his seat, waiting impatiently for the sun to set so the ceremony could begin. In accordance with Jewish tradition, we wouldn't get married on the sabbath, which like all Jewish holidays, ends at sundown. Tyrone and I would stand side by side under an off-white chuppah embroidered in a dark brown thread with the date of our wedding on the Jewish calendar, 30 Tishrei 5770. Rabbi Bernstein would stand before Tyrone and me to give us his blessing, "*Baruch ata Adonai m'sameiach chatan v'kala.*" He'd repeat in English, "Blessed are you Lord who enables the groom and bride to rejoice." The ceremony would come to an end after the Rabbi placed a glass wrapped in cloth on the ground, leaving it for Tyrone to stomp on to shatter the glass. A symbolic ritual, the reminder of the destruction of the Temples in Israel, that out of darkness comes light. The shattered glass, a reminder of the fragility of love and the lifetime it can take to put the pieces back together.

"Mazel tov!" our guests would cheer as they shouted along to the music, while clapping to the beat of "Siman Tov u'Mazel Tov."

Dr. Mohammad 's hand would be grabbed by the older Jewish women who took the lead, bringing everyone together to dance the hora around in a circle, weaving in and out of each other, singing along to "Hava Nagila." As a tall man, standing high above the rest, the men would pull Tyrone towards the center, to support each other as they lifted the bride and groom up on our chairs surrounded by the crowd of dancing guests. Tyrone and I would be bounced around, paraded by the men who held strong below us, trying not to throw out their backs in order to lift us up high above. I would grip tight to the corner of a silk handkerchief, with Tyrone holding on to the other corner. My hands would let go of the chair, not fearing falling to the ground. Our tight knit community of close friends and family would be there to catch us. Tyrone and I could focus on a strong grip of the handkerchief, a symbol of a union, reminding us of the fortitude needed from both ends to stay balanced. An interwoven love as delicate as the silk strings of the handkerchief, our lives together, placed within the grasp of our sweaty hands.

Dr. Mohammad was ever present in my day-to-day life, but my wedding was about surrounding ourselves with the people who would catch us if we fell during all hours of our days, not just nine to five. In the end, no one from the office was invited. If anyone wanted to celebrate, I figured it could happen during business hours.

Ultimately, Dr. Mohammad put formal time aside a month in advance for my wedding send off, the only union that brought us all together for an informal potluck. Dina revealed her pregnancy to Dr. Mohammad a few days earlier, leaving just enough time for Ashley to add another name to the cake, knowing he would not approve another party. Two candles—one pink, one blue—stood tall on a white sheet cake with red swirled icing spelling out, "Congratulations, Jessica and Dina."

A table was set for the entire staff to relish in a celebration, filled from end to end with contrasting flavors intermingling. Each coworker made my favorite dish of theirs. Hala's fattoush, a bright green salad with largely sliced tomatoes, cucumbers, and radishes mixed with green onions, parsley, pita chips, "and a few pinches of sumac," she described of the bright red ground seasoning that added a tartness to the flavor. Abdul Baatin's wife contributed ful sudani, a Sudanese macaroon with roasted peanuts. For sweets, we ate Fatema's gateau au carrot, Ashley's sweet potato casserole, and Liz's chocolate chip shortbread.

Dr. Mohammad had Ashley order hummus, baba ganoush, and pita from Shamshiri Grill in Westwood. But the cherry on the top was the albaloo polo, his favorite dish and one that would become a favorite of mine as well. It was described to me as a Persian dish of stewed sour cherries with saffron basmati rice.

"Do you like it below the knee or around the neck?" Nubia winked, holding a serving spoon above the two meat options, the lamb's shank or neck. The middle eastern delights filled the table alongside macaroni, potato salad, and pecan pie. All of it a treat beyond what the eyes could see.

Imagining honeymoons and travel excited the staff on a topic we could all agree on. "Where would you go?" Nubia asked the group. Anywhere with Tyrone was where I wanted to be. Not wanting to explain we put off the honeymoon, instead, I used "focused on the job and wedding" as my excuse. "Couldn't add a honeymoon to my busy plate." We would wait until life settled down after the wedding—no distractions, no commute, no devices—allowing the only connection to be between each other. I pictured the two of us on a deserted island in the middle of the sea, needing nothing more than each other's company, looking out at the horizon with a future as clear as the waters. The sun would take a bow lowering itself slowly, unobstructed by a single cloud, reaching to the water, signaling a celebration of champagne pink across the sky.

"Fiji?" Dr. Mohammad repeated my response, sounding confused. "Why would you choose Fiji for your honeymoon?" Truly baffled by my choice, he asked, "Do you know where I'd go if I could travel anywhere?" Pausing to consider where the man who flies first class around the world, only to return to a chauffeur who drives him home to his life in Beverly Hills, would want to go? When money is no object, and the ultimate in comfort is available to a religious Kuwaiti man, where would he be most at peace?

"Pittsburgh—it's the greatest place." As his typical glance was respectfully towards the wall behind me, it seemed fitting at this moment that we didn't see eye to eye. The city, unknown for its white-sand beaches, at times didn't even have clean drinking water. The love he found there was brotherly—it was where he met his best friend Buddy, his college roommate, who gave him his first real taste of American pie.

The wedding was upon us, and the office thought my send-off was the perfect time to heed unsolicited advice—a custom my Jewish upbringing had me well acquainted with. "If your love is honey, don't lick it all," Hala announced to the crowd as I put my third piece of baklava in my mouth. "You know, my darling," she looked at me with my mouth full, "there is no sweetness without fire."

"Thank you?" I said, unsure of the message she was trying to send. I squeezed Liz's arm, hoping it would make the divorcés stop talking.

"Fahk...fahk," Nubia shouted. "Mother Fakhfakhina," she exclaimed as Dina brought out a favorite Egyptian dessert, Fakhfakhina, which translated to "the mother of all fruit salads." Glass goblets filled with strawberries, kiwi, and banana covered in mango juice with a scoop of vanilla ice cream. "Cheers," Dina whispered to me, raising the fruit cocktail to clink against mine. With spoons diving into the sweet cups, I felt relieved to have the women chill out for a minute as they devoured what looked like an ice cream float.

"What's your plan?" Liz asked when she knew no one was listening to us.

"We're going to commute daily after the wedding," I said optimistically. "It's fine," I replied to her suggestive look.

"You're not married to your job," she said.

"I can't leave now." I pause. "Anyway, I don't even have a job yet in San Diego. I can't even get an interview." Liz didn't respond. She only listened, hoping instead that I heard my own words. "I have the lease in LA, and Tyrone just rented the extra room out. Remember my friend Leah? She broke up with her boyfriend and needed a place to stay..."

"The friend that drove you to interview?" I nod as Liz asks, "The same one that tried on the wedding dresses?"

★ ★ ★

With twenty-seven stairs left to climb, I heard the bell ring signaling the doors closing for the last train of the day. "Do do do," it chimed. Headed to San Diego to fly with Tyrone to New Mexico for our wedding, I forgot to add extra time to the commute, to lug the extra baggage. Struggling with each step, I used two hands to hoist my oversized suitcase stuffed to the brim. Wrapped in a thin plastic dry cleaning bag, my wedding dress was folded in half and hung over my wrist. As sweat dripped down my arm, it slipped around, forcing my elbow to hold it to my body. I dropped my bags to lunge forward, flailing my empty arm around, trying to keep the door from closing just as it shut. The engineer's arm reached out the side window cueing clearance, while I stood, abandoned on the platform, my white dress flowing from the hot air blowing through the tunnel. Trying to pump the brakes to slow the downward spiral of the thoughts in my head, I took a deep breath in, only to swallow the fumes from the train leaving the station.

When the engineer looked back, to signal the departure, his eyes spotted me on the platform. Holding a fist, he tilted his chin up, cueing me to hop on as he stopped the train to reopen the doors. I believed luck was on my side that day. I had yet to learn that the doors opening for me were part of my privilege, that they were intentionally closed on others.

Nine months from the day I left to say "Till death do us part," a few blocks from the Santa Fe Depot Train Station in downtown San Diego, I would finally learn that luck is not fifty-fifty. When I would see Tyrone's body lying in the road, I would learn that unlike the train, life stops for no one.

Chapter 18

Tied And Bound

*I*n an enchanted land where cowboys saddle up to work their ranches, ballrooms have tin chandeliers and carved wood ceilings. I stood balancing on the tire of a rusted red tractor in a sparkling gold heel as thin as a nail with only a delicate ankle strap holding my body six inches skyward. My hair was pulled to one side, pinned with a piece of antique lace, cut to a length that ended just before it touched my off-white slip dress. Tyrone sat behind the wheel in a sharp suit with the barn behind him, surrounded by acres of lavender. The pathway leading to the farm was lined with cottonwood trees that showed off their age with their magnitude, creating a canopy similar to our chuppah that delicately preserved the passage of space and time. It was October 17th, 2009, at Los Poblanos Historic Inn in Los Ranchos de Albuquerque, New Mexico, a perfect day to get married.

As our guests arrived, they enjoyed sipping lavender lemonade in the gardens, anticipating the dramatic backdrop of colors transforming in the early evening sky. As the sun began to set, the Sandias, the eastern mountain range, would convert to various shades of pink, signaling our wedding could begin shortly that late Saturday afternoon after the Sabbath.

While the guests awaited the big reveal, the ceremony took place in a separate room, away from where an audience could see. Our family, Rabbi Bernstein, and two witnesses stood shoulder to shoulder, encircling Tyrone and me. All in attendance made a commitment to watch over the couple after the Rabbi spoke to the covenant of marriage. "We will comfort and support each other through life's sorrows and joys."

The weight of a heavy black fountain pen was pressed into the hands of the witnesses, passed around for the signing of the ketubah, the Jewish marriage contract.

"Mazel tov!" the rabbi announced, our tight circle repeating after him. "Congratulations!"

"Is that it?" I asked.

Tyrone shrugged, "I've never been married before."

"The rest is for show," the rabbi winked, referring to the practice of walking down the aisle for everyone to see. His words relinquished our bodies to lean back into the soft leather of the couch. My hand rested in Tyrone's. His thumb tucked inward, rubbing the middle of my palm, reminding me he was there. Even when it couldn't be seen, he reminded me to feel his presence.

It was glowing outside under the twenty-foot high covered portal as the glassware sparkled with the reflection of the fire from the tea lights centered around the intentionally scattered wildflowers. Baby artichokes were above each plate, as a placeholder with the name of a guest printed on a small piece of thick cardstock in an elegant font, delicately placed behind the thorn of a leaf. Set as one long table that stretched the entire length of the outdoor patio, one hundred guests would squeeze together intimately, as the maximum capacity was ninety-six. After my mother and I spent hundreds of hours planning every last detail, it came together looking effortless.

"Let's take a photo of the rings," the photographer said as I stood in anticipation next to Tyrone before the ceremony.

"That's okay," I replied with an awkward grin.

"I *always* take a shot of the rings," she stated in a manner that wasn't suggesting there was an option.

"We don't really…" I trail off, glancing at Tyrone to fill in the blanks for me.

"We'll just get a few shots of the rings," she said, disregarding that I was standing there, in my gown that was flowing gently in the breeze of the fall evening, on the patio with turquoise tiles shimmering as the sun highlighted every shade of lavender.

I took the ring off my finger and watched Tyrone do the same as the photographer altered their position to capture them on the only blank spot of the white tablecloth. Instead of looking at the rings, I glanced at Tyrone with a grin that I knew would bring him back to the same moment I was thinking of.

My anxiety was binding. A ring, however, was a decoration wrapped around my finger. The flash blinded us, as the wedding photographer tried to capture what others wanted to see, that size and money sparkle so bright it hypnotized you into believing its commitment. Even with the blinding light of my internal suffering, I could see the beauty of the life ahead of us. "The experience of this sweet life" was inscribed on my simple wedding band. Saying so little and yet so much was just what I needed to hear. When the music began, signaling for everyone to take their seats, I waited in anticipation of walking down the aisle. The irrational fear of my anxiety was like a ball and chain I was unable to let go of. For years, being released to walk down an aisle was unfathomable. Locked around my ankles, its weight dictated how far I could go alone. With fifty feet to get to the end, surrounded by the most intimate circle of friends and family, I still feared crumbling to the ground.

Today, though, I would not let the anxiety have the last dance. I wouldn't let this obstacle keep me from walking down the aisle the way I allowed it to trip me up in life. With not much room to hide anything in my silk gown, in the breast of the dress, I tucked two pills into a cotton ball so they wouldn't disintegrate from the beads of sweat around my neck. As I treaded down the aisle with my parents linked on either arm, I would listen to the encouraging whisper in my head of Tyrone's words from years before: "Pace yourself, Jess." I made it to the end, which was now the beginning.

Chapter 19

Reality Check Not Cashing

Ssssssssssssssssssssss. An ominous sound hissed at Tyrone and me throughout the night as we laid on the floor of my studio apartment on a bustling city street in LA; the sound of a homeless man yelling at a street sweeper was tuned out by the air slowly escaping. *Sssssssssssssss*, it taunted. A week after our wedding, we woke up lopsided when we busted the air mattress Liz let us borrow. She thought it would be a nice break from the futon.

"Get up," Tyrone shouted from the shower, when the first alarm went off at 5 a.m. I was lying on the floor, counting the hours of sleep I was missing. "Get up," he shouted again when the second alarm went off at 5:20 a.m., my cue to put my contacts in, so at 5:25 a.m., I could see Tyrone off at Union Station in downtown LA in my pajamas. Monday through Friday, the first full week after we were married, he rode the train for two hours from LA to Oceanside and then hopped in his car, left at the station, to drive the last twenty-five minutes to work.

Tyrone was on his fifth day of the commute. While he drove us downtown, I dreamed about the forty-five minutes of sleep I would get once I got back to my apartment. I hoped I would find a parking spot since it was a street sweeping day, debating if the price of the ticket was worth the additional rest. A third alarm was already set for 7 a.m. to restart my day and get ready for my next commute, an hour, to get to my office.

With the engine running, he jumped out of the car at the train station while I got into the driver's seat.

"I gotta catch up on sleep," Tyrone said, standing outside of the car, shutting the door from the open window while I buckled myself into the driver's seat. "I'm going to stay in San Diego this weekend." Only married to the daily commute for one week and we were already exhausted.

"Talk later?" I asked. Two words were all it took that day. Leaving one world behind and entering another.

"La la," Dr. Mohammad shook his head no. The spotlight was beaming on his face with such intensity; if his already pale skin turned any whiter, it would be translucent. The only relief would come from the pools of sweat drenching his body and knowing they were concealed by the Armani suit he was wearing. He had feared gathering the staff for so long and was now facing the formidable future. His intimidating stature would no longer serve him. While he was typically hard to read, today, the weakness of his mind was translated on his face, showing the exhaustion from being on constant alert for far too long. His stance was firm, but at this moment, the voice challenging him was stronger. Like drops of water in his ear that came slowly at first but were relentless, flooding his mind into submission. Ultimately, I believe it was the incessant sound that got him to give in. The voice of a nagging Jewish woman. I finally convinced Dr. Mohammad to have our first official staff meeting.

He was outnumbered and would finally be questioned in the spotlight. The man that was twice my size and was a high-level government official—a foreign diplomat—feared sitting in a circle surrounded by women asking him questions. A meeting was perceived as an opportunity to come together to corroborate or commiserate with the potential of creating rebellion and retaliation. Impeding the staff of twelve women and three men assured him short term relief but was creating long term dysfunction for the employees.

I sat on the edge of the seat in front of Dr. Mohammad's desk, which cost more than my yearly salary.

"Dr. Mohammad, come on. It's time," I said.

"I don't understand why you people do this," he replied.

"It doesn't have to be a big deal," I pleaded. "It'll make everyone so happy."

He knew morale was low but couldn't grasp the benefits.

"Why? I don't understand why. Why do you all do this?" He repeated to himself.

The office wanted to have an all staff meeting so they would not have to hear of rumored changes through the game of telephone happening on IM.

"It's like getting your wisdom teeth pulled out," I explained. "It doesn't make sense to only have one pulled. You do them all at the same time, to get it over with. *Your* staff wants to hear directly from *you*." I dreamed that building his confidence and giving him a sense of ownership to the meeting would be a significant contribution.

As if dismantling a bomb, knowing any word could trigger its explosion, I carefully used a gentle voice to seal the deal, "I'll just send a memo out." My intentional nonchalant tone disengaged him and diverted his attention from his ruminating thoughts.

"Fine," he relented.

"Okay," I confirm in a cheery voice, jumping out of my seat, hurrying to prepare the memo before he changed his mind, feeling like my words finally made an impact on Dr. Mohammad.

"It's like adding oil to a machine," I said the previous week, almost laughing out loud, knowing he wouldn't understand I botched the saying, smiling as I realized how much he rubbed off on me. I gabbed on and on to him about the importance of gathering the staff together to build morale, to be transparent, to get everyone on the same page. I reviewed the benefits of open communication and the value it provides the staff. I offered clear objectives that were informative, genuine, and non-confrontational. It took a lot of convincing, mostly based on trust, but that day, I was finally able to persuade Dr. Mohammad to meet with the staff. I was filled with professional pride, as a woman sitting in front of a Kuwaiti diplomat, that he showed faith in me.

Stepping out of his office door, with my back to him, I consciously bit my lip so hard it would hurt. It was an effort to keep from smiling or displaying any visible signs of excitement to avoid alarming the staff. A look of delight while leaving Dr. Mohammad's office signaled the women to be suspicious, triggering assumptions of nepotism. Happiness did not elicit camaraderie in our office. It meant something was up.

I was forcing a straight face, but the professional and personal satisfaction filled my body with a dump of adrenaline. I felt exhilarated—like I didn't even need the shot of espresso that was waiting for me at my desk, now cold from sitting there for hours, most of my morning spent running back and forth to the fax machine. As little as it may have seemed, I believed I was making an impact.

I pulled my chair out from my desk, but before I could sit down, I heard Dr. Mohammad call out down the open corridor.

"Jessica Keith," he yelled out of his office. *Did he just change his mind in the forty-five seconds I took to walk back to my desk?* I speed walked back to his office.

"Yes?" I say to him, now having to force a grin holding my breath.

"I'm just thinking about the memo."

I raise my eyebrows, hoping something about my forced look of positivity will distract him. As if holding onto my breath was a way to keep his word, I wouldn't let it out until I knew he wasn't taking it back.

"On the memo, I think you should…" I heard him say, as I let the air trapped in my lungs release with great relief, his tone confirming the meeting was still on.

"On the memo," he repeated, with a look of glee, like he discovered the missing words in a treasure box, "we will call it," he paused as if hearing a drum roll in his head, "a cupcake party." I stare in disbelief, my lower jaw nearly hitting the floor. "I don't want the staff to think it's about anything too serious," he says with resolve.

Like a child watching her special balloon unexpectedly escape from her grasp, the delight washing off her face, flying out of her hand, out of her control, holding her head up towards the sky, following it until she could no longer see it, I too stood there in disbelief as my pride floated away.

★ ★ ★

"He took the path to hell," Nubia said, "leaving crumbs for Abdul Baatin to find." Fueled by sharing gossip, Nubia worked overtime in the office kitchen to ensure we all heard the rumors about Viraj. Nubia's rumor mill was working faster than ever. "His bite was far worse than his bark."

Viraj left a mark, along with the path that led Abdul Baatin to find money wired fraudulently. While Abdul Baatin kept his head down at his desk, using his hand calculator, Viraj was wiring money to students that weren't studying in the US and cashing out on the unclaimed funds.

"Abdul Baatin caught it all," Nubia whispered sharply. When his ruler didn't line up to match the missing numbers, he pulled out his spreadsheets to see Viraj was cashing out on student accounts who were no longer on scholarship.

"No coin left unturned," Dr. Mohammad yelled from down the hall, standing in the doorframe of Ashley's office. "Count every dinar. Send a memo out," he shouted for everyone to hear.

The ministry would set an example, using this error to question the intent of each employee—tightening the screws on the office door and re-reviewing all personal documents initially sent to the ministry.

"Who has time for that?" Liz IM'd me after getting the message that the ministry would have Dr. Mohammad pay for the embarrassment Viraj caused on Dr. Mohammad's watch.

"Not me," I replied, not knowing I would pay for that later.

At lunchtime, Abdul Baatin stood in the kitchen, hovering over the counter, consuming the microwaved food his wife had prepared for him. With Viraj gone, he spent less time consuming, took more smoke breaks, and worked longer hours. His suit weighed on his body, highlighting his fragile frame; his shoulders hunched over, carrying the weight of the workload.

"Would you like some?" he asked, cupping his hands together underneath the bowl, looking like he was holding out his ration of a brown and gray mixture.

"Smells great," I said politely. "What is it?"

"Liver and onions," he said with a smile. "It's my favorite."

"Oh," I said, "I make a liver dish. I'll make it for you sometime."

For Americans, "sometime" translated as an empty gesture; yet, to Abdul Baatin, I gave him my word. Abdul's eyes lit up bright blue. Surprised by the color that stood out against his dark skin, his shoulders relaxed for the moment as he exhaled a sigh. But Abdul Baatin believed in the words of others, and I was not about to be next in line to disappoint.

"You gonna be okay?" I asked without saying the words "Viraj" or "arrest." They were more than just colleagues. They were in the trenches together. But now Viraj sat in jail while Dr. Mohammad hovered over Abdul Baatin, scrutinizing every penny. Left carrying the weight of their work, along with the betrayal, Abdul Baatin was left to clean up the mess.

"Try it. Please," he said, pulling out an extra fork from the drawer. Again, offering me a bite of his lunch. He needed every calorie in his Tupperware. But I questioned whether it was worse to eat his calories or refuse food from his wife.

"Please, please," he insisted.

I knew we couldn't touch, we couldn't hug, and we couldn't shake hands, but now he was passing me a clean plastic fork to share his lunch, placing a portion on the lid of the Tupperware his wife labeled in Arabic.

"Not what I expected," I said after putting the warm, gray colored meat in my mouth. The dish reminded me of Passover, something we eat to remind us of when Jews were slaves in Egypt. It tasted like chopped liver. I took my fork back from Abdul Baatin's lid and scooped up another bite, this time lopping on the sauce that dripped off the sides. "It's delicious."

On the way home, I decided "sometime" would mean "today." I couldn't erase the sight of the pleasure in his eyes, knowing the pain of the betrayal he veiled. I did what any good Jewish mother would do, stopping at a chic new butcher shop in Los Feliz. McCall's on Hilhurst was one block from my studio, walking distance, where locally sourced organic meat was en vogue. I practiced what I preached, demonstrating kindness within the soul through the liver of a chicken.

The counter showcased meats like duck legs, lamb shoulder, and pork belly in a spotless display that sparkled like a jewelry case at Tiffany's. I eyed the whole beef brisket untrimmed, making a note to self for another occasion. "Can I get a pound of raw chicken livers?"

In my studio, I stood over the sink in a kitchen that was smaller than a coat closet, turning on what looked like an easy bake oven. Washing off the chicken livers, I pulled off some bits, imagining it was strawberries and I was merely plucking the leaves off—the recipe called for searing the meat, roasting, and then grinding it. Without a food processor, a blender used for breakfast smoothies would have to work. After searing the liver, I blended it in small batches like a mixed cocktail but with chicken instead of ice.

"What a treat," Abdul Baatin said the next morning, just happy to have a visitor at his end of the office, unaware of the chopped liver I held behind my back.

"Surprise!" I yelled, pulling out my Tupperware filled with brown mush.

"Oh, Jessica, you did not need to," he says as I hand him the Tupperware.

"It's all for you," I said.

"But Jessica, this is too much. Too kind," he said.

"No big deal," I said, "it was easy." I knew staying up late, taking care in each step, would be worth it the moment I saw his eyes light up, his response as gratifying as I hoped.

"It's all organic," I boasted, "just a few ingredients."

We both smile with mutual excitement. "Mmmmm," he said, taking a whiff, "smells delicious. What's in it?" He reached for a fork wrapped in plastic from his desk drawer.

"Just chicken livers, apples, a little sea salt, and SHIT," I covered my mouth, but the swear word already slipped out. To flavor the meat and keep it kosher, I used Manischewitz, a drink given in small amounts to kids at Passover, tasting like grape juice. *Fuck.* "A splash of wine," I spewed.

The disappointed look on my face cued Abdul Baatin to fill his fork with a huge helping. He closed his eyes and took in a deep breath through his nose. "Mmmmmmmmmm, delicious," he said, not bringing it near his lips. With his chin up, he grinned, "It's as if I had tasted it."

When I returned from lunch, Dr. Mohammad shouted at me, "Shut the door behind you." I sank into the leather chair feeling like a child about to be scolded, waiting for the punishment, wondering if it was all worth it.

"I know," he snapped at me, causing the heat to rise in my body, feeling stuck in the chair while my sedatives rested in my purse, which sat below my desk. I closed my eyes and took deep breaths in through my nose and out through my mouth. It was punishment enough to feel tied to the chair as the panic threatened "death by attack" in silence while Dr. Mohammad yelled. If I looked out the window, I would see how far I was from the Earth's soil and Tyrone's arms. I took a vow, in sickness and in health until death do us part, and here I sat alone.

"I know the truth," Dr. Mohammad hurled at me.

I thought about all the sacrifices I made. I moved to LA without an offer letter. That was enough. I signed a year lease showing my commitment to stay in LA to back pay the taxes I owed for doing this job. That was enough. I got Omar accepted, Abdullah was seeing a counselor, Talal could finish her studies, and Dalia didn't have to live on campus. The list in my head went on and on. "Enough," I said.

"Your lunch," he paused.

My lunch? I thought.

"It revealed everything," he continued.

"I didn't even have lunch today," I said out loud.

"Exactly," he exclaimed, as if that revealed everything. "I saw you outside." Dr. Mohammad paused.

I was outside, I thought to myself. But Dr. Mohammad never took a lunch break in the *year and a half* I worked there. With his eye on everything and everyone after Viraj's arrest, how would he notice me in a busy courtyard, eighteen floors below the window, the corner view of the opposite side of LA?

Dr. Mohammad's paranoia increased every time he received a call from the Consulate's lawyer. Each update revealed a number higher than the last—the amount Viraj stole from the office, wired to an account labeled for a student that wasn't in the US. The rumor mill spilled out that the number was now up to $500,000. While Viraj sat in jail, Dr. Mohammad was in a tailspin, wondering what *his* punishment from the ministry would be.

"I saw it," he snapped. "Traitor," Dr. Mohammad hurled at me. The words intended to sting, instead awoke my spirit from my mind's attack on my body.

I'm not a traitor, I thought. *A compartmentalizer yes, but not a traitor.*

There was something too familiar about his tone. The explosion of his temper, crossing his arms, after he pushed his chair back away from the desk, creating an uncomfortable space between us. His guilt came out in the form of yelling, misplacing his fear with anger. I recognized his loss of control.

With a loss for any other words, my eyes filled with tears while I willed myself not to blink. "I'm sorry," I repeated.

He looked out his window, out in the distance, to get a different perspective.

"I saw you with *her*," he said, unable to look in my direction.

At lunchtime, outside in the courtyard, I strolled along with Dr. Saamia.

"What did you talk about?" he asked, staring out the window. "With the enemy?" He said under his breath.

"Wakeboarding," I replied.

His jaw dropped, turning back towards my direction. "Water boarding?" he shouted.

"No, wakeboarding." During our walk, I learned Dr. Saamia enjoyed being physically adventurous and trying new things. Swerve was too basic for her; she enjoyed more of a challenge. She took advantage of living in Southern California, showing her daughters how to kayak, paddle board, and water ski. I didn't have to ask her "how that worked." She could see it in my eyes, explaining, "We wear a burkini."

The light in the room shone on Dr. Mohammad's pale face, highlighting the fact that he spent all of his time inside at his desk. Dr. Mohammad looked towards me, eyebrows narrowed.

"It's a sport on the water," I explained.

"Do you like your job?" he asked.

I asked myself that every day. I did like my job—it was better than any opportunity I dreamt of. I also knew it was the *only* job offer and it was in LA. In San Diego, despite an endless search, no job found me. I had been at the Consulate for almost a year while the love of my life stuck by my side from 120 miles away.

Dr. Mohammad looked towards me, warning, "Do not go near the honey or you might stick to it."

Chapter 20

Passed Over

"No one is allowed to get pregnant," Dr. Mohammad exclaimed to the nine women that surrounded him at the cupcake party where there was no dessert served. As if we were one of many wives, the women eagerly gathered around Dr. Mohammad in a circle. In this light, he looked pleased with the attractive women he hand-selected for the job, who now surrounded him with bated breath.

"Pretty people make me happy," Dr. Mohammad was rumored to have said to Ashley in confidence. "When they smile, I feel happy." No bright colored lipsticks or skinny jeans showed off or highlighted our physical features. Wearing a "distracting color" of nail polish was against office regulations. Reviewing the health insurance policy, we learned that although no one in the circle wore a hijab, we each had something to hide.

While the women celebrated the review of the health insurance policy, the men stayed put in their designated places.

Abdul Baatin couldn't afford a moment away from his calculator. The chauffeur stood by in the hallway, texting with his wife in Saudi Arabia, waiting for a cue from Dr. Mohammad to order the car from the valet. Nick took the day off to accompany his wife to her six month wellness check at the OBGYN.

The foreigner in our group was an insurance representative brought in to review the health insurance policy details. She was a friend of someone in the Consulate who made money off of selling a package she knew nothing about. Amongst the group of sharp women, her voice sounded dull reading directly off the trifold brochure.

There was a picture of a man with his hands cupped to his ears and a quote in a large font: "Do you hear voices?"

"No one's crazy here," Dr. Mohammad interjected to end the sentence before the woman got any further.

I clicked my tongue at Dr. Mohammad, hoping to get the voice I just heard out of my head. "You might want to rephrase that," I suggested.

"Addiction," she read from the caption under the photo that we could see for ourselves.

"We don't do any of those," Dr. Mohammad said, prompting a laugh between him and the saleswoman, neither of whom knew their audience.

"Dr. Mohammad," I said sharply. Like a mom scolding a child who only needs to hear his name announced firmly to stop what he's doing.

"Are you pregnant?" read a caption below a picture of a woman eating a salad over her growing belly on the next panel.

"No one is allowed to get pregnant," Dr. Mohammad exclaimed to his all-female audience. Dina's hands cupped around her belly, which looked like it was about to burst, her face pale, while the menopausal divorcées flipped the pamphlet to the next page. I glanced at Dina to give her a supportive smile. Dr. Mohammad wasn't put off by Dina's pregnancy yet, as she would work up until the day she gave birth. The pill was too big to swallow—we could be both mothers and professionals. Anything other than working meant less time devoted to him. "She knows she wasn't supposed to do that," Dr. Mohammad said, bringing our attention back to him.

"No, that's not…" I started.

"I specifically asked all of you before you started working here if any of you had plans to get pregnant, and all of you said no," Dr. Mohammad interjected.

Looking at the father of five, I wondered, *What director hires almost all women that are in their childbearing years and expects them not to have children for the sake of the office?*

The meeting should have ended before it ever started. The only thing we learned looking at the shiny trifold health insurance pamphlet was that the saleswoman did not have the plan she brokered. I got what I wanted: a staff meeting. Dr. Mohammad got what he wanted: we all felt like we wasted so much time that we would never ask for another staff meeting.

Eager to debrief everything that transpired, I went to Ashley's office and quietly mouthed to her, "Do you believe this?" looking for anything but a justification.

"We don't abide by American labor laws," she said matter-of-factly, as she always did. Like the students who believed their lies, she said it so many times before we all just assumed it was the truth.

★ ★ ★

Inconveniently for me, Passover fell in the middle of the week, leaving me without enough time or mental resources to get to San Diego and back for the following workday. The Jewish holiday would begin with a Seder, the ceremonial meal that takes place on the first night of the week-long observance. Unearthing a Jewish family to invite me into their home for the holiday in a city like LA—known to be exclusive, expansive, and impersonal—would not be too difficult. Like finding a bagel shop and asking if it serves shmears. Once you locate them, you know the obvious answer. "Hey Leah, does your ex-boyfriend know anyone in LA that would have me over?" I texted a few days before the holiday.

When I arrived at the home I was unacquainted with, it felt familiar. The house was filled with the smell of matzah ball soup and the sounds of children running around in anticipation of searching for the afikomen, a piece of matzah that an adult hides for one lucky child to find. "Eat, eat, eat," sounded like a commandment. Unyielding Jewish mothers find pleasure in nourishing others. My own mother rationalized foie gras by considering it loving to force feed. Unable to avoid meddling, the hostess nudged her unmarried grown-up son to scoot over towards me, the nice, Jewish girl. Lighting the candles, she nudged her son, hoping that where there was smoke, there was fire.

In between the seven courses, she served as the driving force of a yenta, firing off questions in my direction. Her son started to fume, his face turning red, while I sat inches away in the hot seat. "Jessica, what is it that you do for work?" she asked, setting the barometer she would use as a scale to compare to her own children.

"I work for the Consulate of Kuwait," I said, relieved that I didn't have to say I was temping and tell humorous stories from the trenches to entertain the crowd, making everyone laugh while knowing it was at my own expense. Detailing the privileges offered to the students as well as the director, the elderly man at the table turned his head quizzically.

"They use a shofar?" he asked, having trouble hearing me.

"No, no, no, a chauffeur," I explained, emphasizing the "chau."

"Who did you say you work for?"

"The Kuwaiti Government."

The third time I repeated myself, it came through loud and clear.

"You work for Arabs? Don't you know what they've done to us?"

You mean for me? *They gave me a job when no one else would.* "They help thousands of students get an education?"

"I don't understand. How can you do that?"

I know, right? It's so hard to do anything with my anxiety.

"What does your family say?

They brag about it to all of their friends. "They are very proud," leaving off...*that I have a job.*

"You have no business being there," the man snapped at me as I smiled politely, biting my tongue as he continued to wave his finger in my face, "What's wrong with you?" Unrelenting, he dug into me: "How could you bring yourself to do such a thing?"

I gave myself a guilt trip every day—avoiding the mention of my religion in the office, and here I sat at the table with my own, keeping my mouth shut, not saying a word. *What is wrong with* me? *What is wrong with everyone else?*

Uninterested in hearing my response or anything outside of his opinion, he continued, "Young people. So naïve. You never see anything for what it is."

My response didn't matter. I could have explained that Dr. Mohammad was a devout Muslim who prayed five times a day. My favorite quality in him was his faith. Not his religion—rather that he believed in me enough to hire me. During the economic crisis, he offered me something I couldn't afford to turn down, a position of value in my field, something that I prayed for. Dr. Mohammad gave me what no one else had, and that was priceless. It was an opportunity for me to try and see what I could do on my own. I wish in the moment I said one of Dr. Mohammad's truisms: "When our eyes are open to the road ahead of us, we stop looking back." Instead, while pretending to eat the gefilte fish, I found it was just easier to bite my tongue.

Chapter 21

The Icing On The Cake

I stared into the refrigerated display case at the gourmet market, unable to rationalize spending my hard-earned money on my own birthday cake to celebrate in the office. The sticker shock of the overpriced confections taunted me with what little they offered. The first three stores all displayed cakes that would serve five small children—a feast for eyes only—typical for LA, a place where high-priced small portions are illusions of indulgences.

My cosmic fate aligned with the stars on the Jewish lunar calendar. Unlike previous years, my birthday would fall over Passover—the eight days that Jews abstain from leavened foods, which mostly translates to foods with flour like pasta, bread, or other delicious carbs.

A blade that never came near our wedding just six months ago was now making a clean cut, severing the portions between my work and personal life. I wouldn't be able to deny a hand extending a piece offered at my celebration.

When I saw my reflection in the display case, I wondered what it was worth to keep my true identity hidden. The cost was weighing on me as I stared blankly, my eyes whirling beyond what they didn't want to see, denying the reality that I was hiding behind my only option—I would have to find an ice cream cake.

"I'll get it," I said hastily, forcing my voice to sound relaxed, "I'll just pick something up on my way home." Trying to hold back the desperation in my voice, I managed to convince the newly self-appointed birthday monitor that this was my treat. The icing on the cake would be the real surprise—celebrating Abdul Baatin, whose birthday was overlooked during Viraj's arrest.

When my alarm went off at 5 a.m., I didn't waste time getting ready for my special day. I hurried to the office to keep the cheapest ice cream cake I could find from melting on my hour-long commute.

"Want to do me a birthday favor?" I messaged Liz. "Want to get the cake out of the freezer and put two candles in it at 2 p.m.?"

The only treat that day would be seeing Abdul Baatin's face, knowing he wasn't forgotten, getting a glimpse of our names together on a cake we could both eat. The frosted treat that brought us all together awkwardly dazzled, "Happy day Jessica and Abdul Baatin."

"Wait, wait," I shouted, seeing Nahla with a twelve-inch knife in her hand. "Wait for him. Please," I pleaded, the desperation in my voice startling. Nahla passed the knife to Hala behind my back, escaping down the long hallway to let Abdul Baatin know of the "meeting" where his presence was "urgent." To see his overworked face light up would be better than closing my eyes to wish for the fire inside me to stop burning. Like a child sneaking a little taste that no one would notice, Hala licked the icing off her finger. The knife in one hand, the evidence on her other, she winked at Nubia then grabbed a napkin to wipe the deep red frosting from dripping off her wrist. Her fingerprints left a mark across the cake, through the icing, intentionally smudging both of our names all the way through, illegible. A sudden blow to my gut, my face froze in disbelief. Unexpected tears flooded my eyes as I willed myself from blinking, knowing the smallest movement would expose every bit of me. Even with my mind spinning, I could feel the depth of the wound was far below the surface.

I stared at the cake, unable to say a word, while Abdul Baatin stood in the background, his presence unnoticed. A stabbing pain knotted my stomach as the clean blade of the knife taunted. My intentions passed over, severed by the hands of another, I crumbled, wondering why staring at the cake caused *me* such pain.

I heard Hala's voice in the background, making her motive clear to the others, "If the knife is cut through the writing, it will cause harm to the person whose name is on the cake."

★ ★ ★

A text on my phone showed up. "Fired." *What? I'm not even at work. On a Tuesday? On my first sick day? As I sit here alone? Away from Tyrone? Away from my friends.* My thoughts took off, racing faster and faster. *I didn't do anything. I didn't do anything. I didn't do anything.* Like a child, convincing myself I did nothing wrong, my thoughts ruminated on the wheel they couldn't get off. *Compartmentalized. Every. Single. Day. Sacrifice after sacrifice.* I wondered if they would fire me if they knew. The job that gave me every opportunity I needed at a time that I desperately needed it. When no one else would. Dr. Mohammad put his faith in me. *And just like that.*

Another text came through. This time the sender's name caught my eye. The message was from Liz. She knew everything. Everything. "Fired!" I stared at the text, trying to quiet my mind to hear what I was reading.

I woke up exhausted. Everyday. My anxiety took a toll, weighing on my body. I couldn't stomach the day to day; my legs ached, unable to stand the fear that was always looming over me. Not a single sick day used—until that day. "Sick to stomach," I texted Dr. Mohammad the night before, believing some rest might help my system. Wide awake, my heart raced as I laid alone on a futon in my studio apartment, questioning everything.

The phone beeped again. Another message from Liz. "Fatema fired. Can't believe you're not here."

At lunchtime, Liz called to tell me Fatema arrived at 9:15, and by 9:25, she was escorted out the backdoor by two security guards in her high heels, carrying her framed degrees from Stanford under her arm. No goodbyes. Dr. Mohammad's only justification was to Liz, "He who digs a pit for his brother falls into it."

Dr. Mohammad asked Ashley to stay late that night to "look at all the computers for any sticky business." Running updates as she cleared personal files, she was eager to report, "Nothing too sticky" to Dr. Mohammad and to the rest of us, "Porn. Tons of porn."

Ashley was tight-lipped about divulging too many details regarding the criminal charges against Viraj for wiring hundreds of thousands of dollars to unclaimed student accounts and withdrawing them from the other side. However, she was quick to tell us his computer showcased his particular interest in MILF porn.

Nick was too new to know of Viraj's transgressions and that no religion kept the women from judging and scrutinizing the men. Even Nick's conservative ways were not exempt from the scrutiny of the women's evil eye. When Ashley found schoolteacher porn on Nick's computer that night, we all knew he still needed to learn a few lessons.

In the morning, the bright light of the refrigerator highlighted the evidence Nick left for all to see. The women all knew better. Of all the rules that could be broken, this one was transparent. A year and a half ago, when I first started working in the office and saw the sign on the fridge that said "No Pork," I wondered, *Is this like a kosher kitchen?*

Sitting in the fridge for over a week, the see-through packaging of a Lunchables showcased a ham and cheese platter. With the warning "No Pork" on the fridge, no one wanted to be caught with their hands on it. Scotch tape held up the sign that reminded the staff of the dietary restriction.

I knew now what halal was. I just wasn't sure if Nick's genetically modified Lunchables "ham" even included pork as an ingredient.

Liz threw her freshly made fudge into the fridge for us to snack on after a run for our morning coffee. "Go, go, go," I waved her on to hurry out before we were spotted.

"She took the mortar and pestle, mixed it up," Nubia said, motioning like she was stirring a pot, entering the kitchen with Hala, blocking the exit. Hala posted up by the cabinets, pouring the freshly brewed coffee into her Abu Dhabi Flintstones mug. With yesterday's mail folded under her armpit, her hands wrapped around the mug for warmth, the air conditioning vent tossing her hair around.

"Wahda yah makin'?" I chimed in.

The women grinned at each other, then turned towards me, and began laughing. "A baby," Nubia said, swirling her hips in a circle.

I narrowed my eyebrows, not saying a word—not about to fill in the blanks.

"*Yallah*, the Sebou," Nubia explained. "Dina's Sebou. Her baby celebration." Her voice sung out through the hallways, enticing an audience from afar.

"*Aedhirni*, excuse me. Excuse me," Dr. Saamia said, bumping into Hala to get a good seat in the standing room only space. Hala held tight to her coffee, spilling the mail to the floor. Seven other females filled into the tight space. There was nothing we all agreed on with few exceptions. "Baby" and "celebration" were two words that brought us together faster than a fire drill.

Abdul Baatin stepped into the door frame, glancing past the women, his eyes and grin directed at the coffee pot. The scent of the earth brewing swirled with the Calvin Klein perfume Dr. Saamia was doused in. Abdul Baatin took two steps backwards, an empty coffee mug in his hand. Hala raised her eyebrows. "Not thirsty enough?" She laughed, cheering her full mug in the air. Abdul Baatin cheered his empty mug, looking defeated, and turned back towards his office.

"They put the baby in a sieve. A kitchen sieve," Nubia explained in slow detail the Egyptian tradition of welcoming a baby on the seventh day of life. "Of course, the baby is shaken in the sieve. Of course."

"Dina's grandmother, she bangs copper pestle against the mortar. You know?" she asked, looking to see if we knew how to fill in the blanks.

"To rid the spirits."

Dr. Mohammad passed by, stopping at the kitchen that he never entered. His presence silenced the women, yet he froze, like a deer caught by a pack of cougars. Hala's eyes, outlined with a smokey black liner, glared at him, creating heat from the women's attention towards his body, signaling a fire to Dr. Mohammad. "Something terrible happened?" he asked.

"Dina's baby's here!" Nubia shouted.

Dr. Mohammad's pale face exaggerated the hint of rose coloring his cheeks. He took a handkerchief from his pocket to wipe the sweat off his balding head, taking a deep breath in through his nose, no longer smelling of his fear, his shoulders dropped down, letting out a sigh of relief.

"Yes, so terrible," he paused, shaking his head. "So terrible, she's not at work… She's missing all the fun."

His smirk cleared the kitchen of what he considered child's play.

"Let's get outta here," Liz said, tilting her chin up to exit the front door. She mouthed "coffee" with her bright pink lips.

I nodded, knowing I needed a jolt. I was tired of the same thing every day and done with eating matzah. I longed to feel like our time wasn't dictated or restricted by the unstated expectations and regulations set for the staff at the Consulate of Kuwait. I knew pushing the envelope, being away from the office too long, made Liz nervous, but I needed a change of scenery. I pushed the heavy glass doors to exit the tower and started running, pulling her by the hand. Without losing any time, we made it fifty feet across the lawn to the adjacent tower. Our break, in reality, was feeling the fresh air against our faces as we left to get coffee across the plaza at the Coffee Bean and Tea Leaf.

Standing in line ahead of us was Liz's celebrity sighting, Sal Masekela, an African American host on *E!* and *The X Games*. While tourists wear their Beverly Hills t-shirts and pay top dollar to be driven around on a double-decker British bus to get a glimpse of a private driveway, for LA dwellers, saying hello to a star was like wearing cowboy hat to see a hip hop show—it broadcasted to everyone that you were not from this neck of the woods.

Attempting to play it cool, I placed my post-Passover order, a toasted bagel with schmear. After ringing me up, the hurried barista brought back the remnants of what looked like a bagel used to put out a fire.

Uninterested in being a bother and assuming most of her patrons were high maintenance, I was self-conscious of Sal standing at the register next to me. "The bagel is *black*. I can't eat a *black* bagel," I blurted out. "I can't eat a *black* bagel," I repeated.

Sal's eyes looked in my direction. The heat from his glare burned right through me, while the word "burnt" escaped my vocabulary. He rolled his eyes and looked back at the barista serving him, tilting his head to point out the mess I was making with my words. Liz's face beet red, she held the door open with her foot to help me make a quick exit, coffee in one hand, waving frantically with the other, hoping to catch my attention without causing a scene.

I couldn't stand the thought of Sal Masekela, a total stranger, judging me judging a bagel.

Liz mouthed "No" in slow motion, "Do not…" shaking her head, watching me walk towards Sal, to her dismay, believing you never address famous people. As if we would turn to stone by speaking to them.

I mouthed "Fine" back to Liz, the words washing the look of embarrassment off her face.

Pretending to admire the untoasted bagels in the display case, I took a step away but then swirled around on my heels, reached out a finger, and gently tapped Sal on his forearm.

"Hey there," I said, pretending not to notice the horror on Liz's face. "Do I know your father?"

In that brief moment, I broke every rule in our office. Touching a man, questioning him, and speaking of his family. He looked at me bewildered, our minds racing in separate directions.

I couldn't stop myself. "Is your dad Hugh?"

"Yeah?" he replied.

"How's your family doing?" I asked, imagining his thoughts working overtime to determine if he somehow knew me.

"Good?" Sal responded. His look mirrored Liz's, bewildered by who I was and what I was asking. Accustomed to being approached by strangers interested in his stardom, my words spun in circles, dizzying him with confusion.

I decided to interpret his look of consternation as an assumption that I wouldn't recognize him as the son of Hugh Ramapolo Masekela, a South African jazz musician, whose music received international acclaim protesting apartheid.

"I listen to your dad's music," I nod to him, while hoping it translates to "I hope you don't think I'm racist." The gratification I thought I'd taste was more like the burnt bagel—not what I hoped for.

The barista yelled out my name, interrupting my internal dialogue. As if I'd see Sal next year at High Holy Day services, I said, "Hope your family's doing well," grabbing my bagel and schmear to go.

★　★　★

While the sun shined year-round through the sparkling windows of our LA office, I kept a winter coat on the back of my chair. The air conditioning, always on full blast, kept my body from signaling that it was on fire. *Take off your top*, I told myself when the heat continued to rise in my body. Taking off a long-sleeved sweater, which was buttoned up over a thin camisole, wouldn't work. Breaking the dress code was not an offense I was willing to make. Removing another layer would be revealing too much. Staring out the window, seeing dots of colors moving so far below, reminded me that, similar to anxiety, people can't see what's happening on the inside. The heat continued to rise as an alarm rang in my ears. The piercing sound alerted my system to reach for my purse. After staring outside at the light of day, the inside seemed darker as I put my head below my knees underneath my desk. I blinked my eyes hard, waving my arms, trying to feel around.

"You're dying right?" I heard Liz's voice ask from above, hitting my head coming up from underneath my desk. I spun around on my chair to see her in a short-sleeved shirt, her sweater tied around her waist, beads of sweat around the nape of her neck. She held out her cell phone and shined a light at my feet so I could see her grab my bag. "Electricity's out," she said, which had caused the fire alarm to go off.

"Let's get out of here," she said, grabbing me by the hand, helping me up.

With the elevators turned off, the death trap couldn't save me; an exit sign pointed to a stairwell. A discreet door opened up to an endless shaft of concrete walls. The prestige of a suite so high up felt like a punishment, the endless stairs, a reminder that the pathway to purgatory is often paved by people who believe they are above it all. I stared at the ground trying to focus on each step, one at a time, with fear that looking ahead would seal my fate.

As the temperature in the dark narrow space continued to rise, others were in an inferno, seeing red, charred by the sun's ability to burn. I blinked my eyes open, seeing the stairwell filled with people. The desperation on too many faces stood out as a reminder that many in that stairwell upended their roots to replant themselves in LA, where they found themselves yet again running out of a twin tower.

The number of people filling the tight space increased with each step. As people pushed by, nearly knocking the wind out of me, I closed my eyes and froze. *You are a tree.* I told myself. *You are a tree. I am a tree. I am a tree feeling a breeze passing through my branches.* When I heard the steps around me, rushing by my limbs, it sounded of an eagerness to run through the crackling leaves of the fallen. The heat came from the warmth of the sun, its rays circling around, reaching all the way down to the bottom of my roots, buried deep into rich soil, reminding me to feel the growth as the brightness shined through as a reminder of resilience, the ability to keep growing.

Chapter 22

Luck And Lies

"Vacation's over," Nahla smirked at Dina on her first day back from maternity leave. Twelve weeks after having her first baby, she stepped gingerly into the office, a stain from her venti cappuccino down her shirt.

The rest of the women wanted to hear her tales of survival, of early days in the trenches of motherhood. "At lunch," Dina grinned. "The bigger babies need my attention," she said, referring to the students, opening her email to see what she missed. Three thousand new messages stared back at her. An IM from Nahla popped up on her screen. "I couldn't do *all* of your work. Had my own."

"I've answered five emails and 150 text messages so far," she said at 9 a.m. Her husband, who was taking care of the baby "on his own" with his own mother by his side, sent more requests per minute than the students had in three months. "WHERE ARE WASHCLOTHS?" He texted as if his life depended on it. The workload she knew how to manage. But the demands at home now fought for her attention.

Dina skipped lunch at noon to speed home to feed the baby and to make a sandwich for her husband. Returning to the office out of breath, rushing to collapse onto a pillow placed on her chair, her phone back in her lap. "Leisurely lunch?" Nahla scoffed, looking at her watch, then swirled around on her heels, turning her back to Dina, pushing through the heavy doors to the office suite, heading outside for a smoke break.

Dina's head dropped down, to read an alert from her cell phone, distracting her from her stomach growling, hungry for the lunch she didn't have time to eat. "CLEAN BOTTLES?" her husband messaged.

At five o'clock, Dina dragged herself down the long hallway to give Dr. Mohammad updates on her student cases. Since the early days of the office when it first opened, Dina cared for Dr. Mohammad, responding to his every demand in a tone that put him at ease.

"You're back to care for me?" Dr. Mohammad said.

"I'm done."

"Inshallah, we see you tomorrow."

"*Halas*," Dina repeated, "I'm done."

It only took three months and eight hours for Dina to acknowledge she couldn't care for everyone.

"And without you?" Dr. Mohammad asked, wondering how he would manage. Now with an office of advisors filling the cubicles, he remembered she was there from the beginning, when there was no one to fill the seats.

Leaving his office, for the last time, she replied with Dr. Mohammad's words, "Put the pacifiers in their mouths and let them suck it."

★ ★ ★

Three months later, Dina's position remained unfilled. It was neither posted nor approved by the ministry to hire a replacement.

"He can't afford to lose me now," Nahla said with a job offer in hand, ready to leverage it for higher pay, a better title, and fewer caseloads. Dr. Mohammad was positioned right where she wanted him—distraught from Viraj's misappropriations, rattled by Dina's departure, and exhausted from the incessant demands of the ministry.

"He'll pay for it," she smirked, heading down the hall, her head high, standing tall in her heels, looking down on the rest of us.

"Inshallah, he'll call her bluff." Hala narrowed her eyebrows. But we all knew Dr. Mohammad crumbled in desperate situations. Believing she was now his favorite child, he would offer whatever pacified her needs. The door was left open for all of us to hear. She wouldn't negotiate; she would dictate her demands, drawing out her conditions to stay or leave. He sat in the hot seat while she stood her ground. Like a child being scorned, Dr. Mohammad looked away from Nahla's heated words toward the view out the floor to ceiling windows. Downtown peeked out from a smog covering, like the cloud that hung over the rest of us.

Nahla took a breath from her argument, offering him the pause to agree to her terms. His response to seal the deal:

"Like selling your goods on the street for money, your efforts are needed outside."

★ ★ ★

Before Tyrone arrived for the weekend, I took Liz's advice and made a dinner reservation online to avoid the maître d' asking, "And you are?" with her nose stuck up in the air. Rolling her eyes when I said, "We have a reservation," she couldn't do what she believed was her job: letting only the who's-who in.

On Saturday evening, Tyrone and I drove the nine blocks from my studio in Los Feliz to Cafe Stella, a French bistro in the neighborhood. Two men in black suits stood in front of the "$20 Valet Parking" sign that stood out in front of the restaurant. Tyrone pulled the car up and reached into the middle console to grab a handful of loose coins to fill the parking meter on the street just two spaces in front of the valet.

I took off my sunglasses to see the transformation from a sunlit evening in LA into a dimly lit bistro with red brick walls and black velvet curtains. An easel held up a chalkboard with cursive swirling, "Le Menu Du Jour," spelling out the specials of the day in French that painted a picture for the imagination, omitting the practicalities of listing prices. A star-shaped glass window gave a glimpse for the staff to peek through the double swinging doors from the kitchen. Waiters wished through the star that the next table they serviced would be their big break. Disappointment was finding mere mortals, who took up time enjoying their food in lieu of posing over a $120 Bordeaux.

"Do you have wine by the glass?" Tyrone asked.

"Just water for me, please." I smiled at the waitress.

Unimpressed by our drink order, the waitress smirked back. Believing we had nothing to offer her, she hurriedly asked, "Ready to order then?"

"I'll have the steak frites please. Medium rare." When I looked up from the menu, the waitress smiled, her posture taller. Reaching into her pocket she grabbed a lipstick and outlined her thin red lips with a bright pink, going far beyond the boundaries, to plump up the appearance.

"Will that be all?" she asked before Tyrone even ordered. My eyes narrowed, tracing her glance, which was directed at the table next to us. Jeremy Piven, the star of the HBO hit show *Entourage*, was seated comfortably at the bistro table inches away. Across from him sat a woman with long, blonde extensions who stood six feet tall with white, strappy, stiletto heels that tied crisscrossed up her legs. Her augmented lips, highlighted with a bloodred lipstick, looked swollen from fresh injections. A champagne-colored, mini, slip dress barely covered her bottom when she sat down.

"A bottle of Veuve," Jeremy asked without looking up to see if there was a waiter to serve him.

While looky-loos at surrounding tables wrenched their necks to get a peak of the Hollywood star, I avoided eye contact with his date, feeling too judgmental to glance in her direction. I whispered to Tyrone, "She doesn't look Jewish."

"Seriously?" Tyrone asked, unimpressed by the sight.

"I know. Doesn't matter. But I read in *People* magazine his mother wants him to marry a nice Jewish girl."

A candle melting between us shone a gentle light on Tyrone's face. His eyes looked straight into mine, igniting the flame within me that warmed my heart anytime I saw a grin fill his face. I watched his dark lips as he whispered, "I lucked out."

★   ★   ★

"Lies. All lies. They will pay for every last one," Dr. Mohammad said a few months back. "They were not who I thought they were," he spewed to anyone who walked into his office, each time Ashley prepared a memo to notify the ministry of Viraj, Fatema, or Holly's transgressions.

His words ruminated in my head when I found an empty green file labeled "Mohamad al Jabari." Surrounded by folders stuffed to the brim, overflowing with documents, and every email printed out, a name I didn't recognize stared back at me. There was no verification of enrollment, no transcript, and no copy of a passport stamped with a date of entry.

The only other place I found his name was on the approved list of students who receive their salaries. The error snowballed as I reviewed the memos sent to Abdul Baatin to release the funds to the student whose name was on the list. Book allowance. Clothing allowance. Salary. As I looked through my records, I discovered I paid him on time and in full over the past seven months. The one file that slipped through the cracks was a $47,000 error that I believed would cost me everything.

Viraj, Fatema, and Holly all paid for their errors. I couldn't decide what punishment would be the worst. They could fire me, leaving me with a year lease, no job, and still paying the taxes I owed without an income. Or they could keep me in the office working overtime until I could pay back every last cent. If I ever got a job offer in San Diego, my debt would tie me to LA even longer, keeping me away from the life I was dying to live with Tyrone. My lack of work-life balance was payback enough.

"Go tell him," I yelled at myself, as I shook my head. "No way." I grilled myself, "What took you so long to find this error?"

"You'll pay for this," I heard Dr. Mohammad say in my head. "You're not who I thought you were."

I wondered how long it would take them to find the error I was holding in my hands. If I just put the file back in the cabinet, no one would know. In this office, when I tried to do the right thing, it was always wrong—every time. I didn't cry over spilled milk with the tiramisu, the cupcake party, or the chopped liver debacle. Of all the things I regretted, it was not saying a word when I should have.

I ran to Dr. Mohammad's office, fighting the urge to keep it a secret, sweating before I even got to the hot seat.

"Oh God. It's bad. Oh God," the words I couldn't hold back, spilled out flooding my mouth, not making any sense, not wanting anyone to hear.

Dr. Mohammad's face was pale, looking towards me as if I was a teenage girl with no mother around, left to her father to take care of a problem he was not ready to deal with. His cheeks blushed, his face becoming a darker red as I sat across from him with my legs crossed, on the edge of my seat.

"La, la, la." He waved his arms and shook his head. "Maybe one of the ladies could help you," he said, fearing what was to come. He wasn't ready for the words flowing out of my mouth like a volcano as I erupted.

"Wired money. Student not studying. Not in the US. Forty-seven thousand dollars," I spewed the mistake I made, leaving Dr. Mohammad to fill in the blanks that he would have to relay to the ministry. Every mistake was a reflection of him. His name. His burden. He would pay for it "out of his own pocket," I remembered him saying when I first started working for him.

I believed I knew Dr. Mohammad. His every move predictable. Yet I could never have imagined his response. "It was an honest mistake," he said.

He stood up, cuing me to go get the empty file before calling Abdul Baatin to help him account for the missing money.

"Remember not to close the door," he paused.

"I know, Dr. Mohammad," I said.

"No, no, you don't. Not yet," he said, letting out a sigh. "Do not close the door on what brings in wind. Let it blow off."

★ ★ ★

"Train's late," Tyrone texted. I was already in my studio apartment when I got the message. We were testing out a new plan, and this was our trial run. I ended the first part of my sixty-minute commute down Sunset Boulevard from Culver City to Los Feliz, leaving my car parked in front of a U-Haul station in two-hour parking just around the corner from the metro stop at Vermont and Sunset. I changed out of my work clothes in the car and into my running gear to jog the last mile home. Tyrone planned to take the train to the metro to meet my car with his spare key then drive the last mile back to my studio. Our well-executed plan came to a halt. "We're not moving," Tyrone texted. "Stuck on the train."

Safe at home, my mind started to spin, the walls caving in; my mind interpreted "stuck" as "trapped." I grabbed my keys and headed back down the hill to my car. Outside, the voice in my head was drowned out by the noise pollution on the crowded streets where cars banged on their horns for the cars ahead to move inches forward. I drove my car the mile back up and circled the block for twenty minutes, waiting for someone to leave their two-hour parking spot, a safe space from 8 p.m. to 8 a.m. "Still here," Tyrone texted to give me an update. The two-and-a half-hour train ride would arrive four hours late. "Phone's about to die," his last message came through. By 11 p.m., when Tyrone's train was expected, I headed downtown to Union Station to greet him. There wasn't as much traffic, making the hour-long drive fifteen minutes.

I parked on the southside of the station and entered through the back. Passengers leaving the train platform were greeted in the dimly lit station, in the dark of the night, by friends and family. I stood alone waiting for Tyrone. A pounding in my heart drummed through my ears until it was loud enough that I could hear the noise outside of my body. I plugged my ears with my thumbs, wrapping my hands around my eyes to cover the lids that were tightly shut. Standing in silence, I tried to escape the sounds in my head. When I released my hands, my soul felt like it was being pulled by the pounding sound, directing my eyes up to the drumming now outside of my body. Tyrone was locked inside the train. He banged on the window to get my attention. Barely visible in the darkness of the train, he was left inside.

After I notified an engineer of my passenger on the train, he unlocked it without a care or an apology to Tyrone, who had fallen asleep and went unnoticed when the train was shut down and locked up for the night.

"No worries," Tyrone said, looking at me with a smile, to calm *me* down. "I'm all good."

We sat in silence for the ride home, both of us exhausted by the day. I circled around the block a few times before we found a parking space. We made it to the studio by midnight and collapsed onto the futon. Tyrone set his alarm for 5 a.m. I turned mine on for 5:20 a.m. "I could have slept on the train," Tyrone joked before he dozed off.

The alarm went off in what felt like five minutes later. I was so tired in the morning that I barely remembered what happened the night before. The five hours asleep together was not time well spent. I was literally driving in circles, getting on the on ramp after dropping Tyrone off back at the station. With no sign of parking back at my studio, I left my car in a yellow zone and unloaded my body back to bed.

Driving down Sunset on the way to work sixty minutes later, I diverted my eyes to avoid staring at the nearly naked bodies on a Calvin Klein ad. The billboard displayed an image of an office bathroom. A man stood shirtless, leaning up against a woman, looking beyond her eyes, one knee exaggeratedly pointed out, twisting his body to use what looked like the strength of his pelvis to trap her between his legs, forcing her body against his bare skin, pleats forming in his crotch to show off his pleasure through the bulge in his pants. The image of the man stared back at me, hoping I noticed, wondering what it would make me do. The spectacle pulled me in, wanting me to look while making me feel like it was wrong. An undressed body crossed a line far beyond breaking rules of a religion that wasn't my own, but just like the others, I chose to stay in my lane.

I could see the next six stoplights ahead, all glowing red. When the lights turned green, it didn't signal drivers to move forward. The road was too crowded, outnumbered by the swarms of cars. The signal to go taunted its audience that was held captive, surrounded by larger-than-life billboards—the eye candy that pacified the passersby with something yummy to look at. The black-and-white image plastered up in front of me wanted to be a spectacle. The breathless figures looked hungry, but I wasn't interested in what they were having. I didn't need to be religious to feel the need to look away. There were so many messages plastered around me on the drive to work, most of which suggested a barely-clothed skinny body was the means for survival in this town.

Unlike the billboard, which suggested leaving nothing to hide, I now found it more comfortable to sit fully covered at the office. Survival in my world was managing the commute and the elevator ride, which depleted my body, and rewarding myself with chocolates from Liz's file cabinet.

Arriving at work, I walked down the hall with my head up, staring back at the portraits of the royal family, feeling like we almost saw eye to eye. Turning on the computer, I wondered what email requests I would be able to smile at, now understanding the message the students were trying to get across.

"You've been warned," the first email sent two minutes ago stated. My stomach dropped while my mind raced, wondering who even noticed me arrive on time without a coffee on a few hours of sleep. I had only walked from the elevator to my desk and sat down. "SUBJECT: Change and return." The email read, "You have officially been issued a warning. Your attire does not meet the code of conduct implemented in our office." The email was from Ashley. I blinked my eyes hard, wondering if the exhaustion from the commute had me misreading signals. "Future warnings of this sort will lead to harsher repercussions. Jeans do not meet the dress code. You have been warned. Two hours of vacation time will be deducted for you to return home to change."

I was wearing Banana Republic pleated trousers with a tailored leg cuffed at the bottom and an orange cashmere sweater over a long, white, button-down blouse. The outfit was a purchase specifically for this job, so I could be covered in a fitting manner.

Seriously? I couldn't stand the idea of being punished by anyone other than myself. I tested the limits with a real error that cost Dr. Mohammad, who paid it forward, proving to me my job wasn't on the line. Ashley's email, however, was a misuse of time and perceived power. It was the unwritten message that was sent and received. My body flooded with adrenaline, driven by fear. All I could think about was the last twelve hours, all of the driving I survived. I would surely go off the rails if Ashley sent me home to change my pants and return to the office. Just the thought of it would be enough to drive me out of my mind, on a trip that was just around the corner.

After I had walked in place for an hour on the treadmill of my apartment complex in San Diego in February of 2002, it had measured farther than my steps outside in months. My body was strong, but my mind was stronger, cynically, to my demise. It was in control and had taken over my every move, as a passenger strapped into a rollercoaster, along for a ride I didn't want to be on but couldn't get off. No words went together in any order that made sense to anyone, including myself. The thoughts illogical and incoherent—and yet so loud. I was paralyzed by fear; going outside of a five-mile radius was too far away from my comfort zone. My thoughts punished me with a pain so great, I momentarily understood why some see death as a relief.

Driving anywhere, I felt the steel surrounding me as if it was pushing on my chest, keeping me from taking full breaths. The panic sat in the driver's seat, telling me that I was trapped in the car and couldn't get out. The voice in my head screamed, "*You are going to die, and no one can help you.*" My dry mouth tasted like metallic cotton balls waiting to absorb the hot yellow bile bubbling in my throat. My nose filled with the fumes from the cars around me, flooding the air, leaking into my lungs. The only thing holding me together was the seat belt that cinched around my body, making me feel like I was trapped to an electric chair. The lightness in my head made it too unstable to even hang over the wheel. My fight or flight response had pumped adrenaline through my veins. With great urgency to want out of my own body, the voice in my head had screamed so loud, making my limbs tremble, "*You are going to die, and there's nothing you can do about it.*"

Oh no. Not this time. I told myself, forcing my eyes to blink hard to focus on the office space that surrounded my body—not to look back, for reality was in front of me. I had come too far to go back to that place. I rushed to the bathroom, slipped the lock on the stall, and swallowed hard on the bile that rushed to my throat. I pulled down my pants and rested on the toilet seat, lowering my head between my knees. I kicked my shoes off to cool my body down. My eyes tried to focus on the back label of my pants. Staring down the leg of my trousers, my eyes tried to focus on the tag, branded with what it was made of. A loose thread taunted my calf with a tickle. In one quick snap, I tore the dangling fiber off. The label stayed on—it wasn't hanging by a thread, and neither was I. We all knew Ashley was smart, but no one needed her to sign her Post-It notes with PhD at the end to remind us. She persuaded Dr. Mohammad to limit her caseload and transition into a position with authority over her peers. She still needed to learn that respect and compliance would not be a given from the overworked, resentful advisors that took on her cases, offering her more time to google "how to be effective in the workplace."

Without the burden of work, she created her own set of rules. A shiny new binder sat on her desk that contained new regulations she imposed on the staff. A warning issued meant an employee did not abide by the new manual of regulations. Three issued warnings prompted probation. Adding rules and punishments to grownup type As with X chromosomes would inevitably receive resistance leading to a plan B.

Her manual stated, "Everyone is required to arrive and leave at the same time," but she was the exception to the rule. "Everyone is issued the same number of caseloads," yet she was the exception to the rule. "You are required to report all sick and vacation hours." Her manual made it clear to the staff that the rules did not apply to her. Favoritism was easier to swallow—unlike the rules, it wasn't new to the staff.

I didn't need a PhD to defend my case. Ashley's infractions were going to be used against *her*. Typing with vigor, I emailed my reply: "It has been brought to my attention that the following infractions have also been made within our office: 1) Leaving early, 2) Unequal distribution of caseload, and 3) irregularity in reporting of sick and or vacation time.

It would not be ethical to issue warnings unless doing so equitably. Furthermore, until this policy is issued consistently, as a matter of principle, I will remain in my conviction to wear the pants that may seem denim in color but in actuality are trousers." Without falling to pieces, I stood my ground.

A reply email came through a minute later: "As a one-time courtesy, you won't be sent home to change."

"Coffee break?" Liz IM'd.

"Too tired," I responded. I turned my chair around to face the light out the window, my back to the open door. Receiving the warmth of the sun, I wondered what I was doing here. With no time to dream, I closed my eyes.

When a cup hit my desk and the words "Two hot shots" came from Liz's voice, I re-awoke to my reality. "Two hot shots of espresso that is." Not waiting for me to bring my cup up to hers, she cheered her cup to mine, placed on the desk. "We got this," she said, responding to the defeated look on my face.

I took a sip from the warm cup, my usual drink, but what I held in my hands didn't feel like what I wanted.

★ ★ ★

On a Friday, I checked my flip phone to see if Tyrone texted, hoping he would catch an early train.

"Little Dom's?" Liz said, tapping her finger on her iPhone to make a dinner reservation for two on Saturday night. "Eight's open." Without looking up or needing my reply, Liz tapped away so I wouldn't have to use my old-fashioned method of calling around to secure a seat at an open table for two.

"It's two blocks from your apartment," she added. Like a good Jewish mother, she showed me her love by ensuring Tyrone and I would eat well. "Try the meatballs," she said after securing a plan for the only night of the week that my relationship wasn't in transit.

My phone beeped, alerting me to a text. "Catching late train." I closed my eyes, wishing I misread the message, hoping that when I reopened them, I would see clearly. I lifted my chin towards the sun, appearing to capture some rays of light on my untanned skin but really drying up any tears before they escaped. With my eyes shut, I felt the warmth of the sun against my hand, letting me know it was there, shining bright on me. Drying my tears would be our secret. I opened my eyes to see Liz's hand rested on top of mine. "Trust me," she said, "you'll love the meatballs."

A neon sign for Little Dom's stood out from the aqua green and black tile, framing the large windows with black and white striped canopies that hung over the sidewalk tables covered in butcher paper and squeezed closely together. Inside, hipster bartenders in bow ties showed off their skills stirring dirty martinis, entertaining the patrons in oversized leather booths, seating an older audience far away from the scene outside.

Tyrone stood tall in front of his folding chair with a giant grin on his face, watching me squeeze by the table next to us, sucking in, trying to avoid letting my bottom knock over a wine glass. A woman, her wrist locked up with gold Cartier bracelets, reached her French manicure for her purple ostrich leather clutch, removing it from my chair, annoyed that it no longer had a seat to itself. "Pardon me," I said. Since the woman's gaze focused on her date, I found myself speaking directly to the purse. I slipped into the folding chair, looking up to see Tyrone waiting for me to get comfortable before taking his seat.

That's Kate Bosworth. I stared at Tyrone. *Hollywood star Kate Bosworth.* I tried to shout with my eyes.

"What's up?" he asked.

I knew he would be more interested in our date than the one happening next to us. "Wanna share the fresh catch and meatballs?"

"An interesting combo." Tyrone looked weary of my choice. "Sure. Whatever you want."

"Can I offer you something to drink, sir?" the waiter asked Tyrone.

"An old fashioned, please," he said to the waiter and then looked back at me. "Do you ever think about us living in LA together?" Tyrone asked.

But my attention was back on the couple. My eyes followed the waitress, eager to learn what she had to offer. Her arm reached out, placing a large white plate sprinkled with frisée leaves in front of the famous star seated inches away, across from a man who appeared more interested in his martini than anything else. I looked up from her plate, cringing at the sight of her collarbone standing out like a hanger holding up a sheer, soft pink silk blouse. She used one hand to push the frisée around on her plate, using her other arm like a wand, turning her wrist filled with the gold bracelets, which clinked as they dangled around, trying to charm her date.

I felt a tightness in my chest as I glanced at hers. She resembled a painted glass fish swimming in an aquarium—two lines of bright colors catch your eye as the transparency of the body mesmerizes with its illustrious glow. Yet a closer look shows a body so thin, injected with artificial dyes, showcasing the fish trapped behind glass, appearing more attractive for entertaining an audience.

"Jess?" Tyrone repeated. "Do you ever think about what life for us would look like living in LA?"

"The daily catch?" the waiter interrupted, looking to set the hot plate down on the table. He balanced the meatballs in one hand and the fish in the other. A warm breeze wrapped around our table, lifting the smell of the butter swirling with the garlic, floating up from the crackling red snapper.

I stared straight into Tyrone's eyes, without saying a word, shaking my head. I no longer had any interest in the fish.

Chapter 23

The Big Bang

*E*xhausted by my everyday routine, I counted down to celebrating the Fourth of July in San Diego. The long weekend couldn't come soon enough. I was eager to catch up with my friends and was curious about what was going on when Leah texted, "need to talk." The text caught me by surprise in the middle of the workday while I was waiting in Dr. Mohammad's office for a signature, unable to respond.

"Look what I have done," Dr. Mohammad said to me when I looked up from reading the text message. Reaching his arm out in front of my eyes, I only noticed the grin on his face that shone through. Typically, both of his shoulders were raised up, attempting to keep a phone on each ear, listening to two conversations at once. As if playing twister, right hand on a pen, left hand holding the paper down and moving his chin upward and to a side to his assistant to note when and where she should place her hand to pull the phone away from his face.

I didn't need to look at the image to see what he accomplished. The bustling advisors now filled the office that once didn't have desks. Cubicles were readied before any new staff was brought on. They didn't have to sit at the conference table for weeks waiting for a computer, paper, and a pen. There were now official email addresses, passwords, and a server to share and protect student data. With all of the orders he was given from the ministry, showing off the photo reminded him of what he accomplished on his own.

"Look what I did," Dr. Mohammad squealed with delight. "Sent to my wife."

Dr. Mohammad's family had left LA to go back to Kuwait for a summer vacation. He was at home alone to survive the two weeks with only his driver, butler, maids, a tea boy, and the children's tutor. "I am all alone," he said, "and I made this." His shoulders rolled back, his posture higher in his chair, the light shining through the glass windows behind him, sitting in his corner office far above the ground. He flipped his cell phone open to show off his accomplishment.

"I think you're on the wrong one," I said.

The photo showed Dr. Mohammad, the camera turned around, facing him showing his large hands holding an open pizza box that covered his body. "Nom, nom," he nodded his head, sounding like Cookie Monster, eager for his treat, "I just want to take a bite." I looked at him, uncertain as to why he would show me the picture on the screen and why it was meant for his wife. "Delicious, no?" He reached his arm back out for me to get a better look. "So kind on the eyes, so good on the tongue." Standing in the kitchen of his Beverly Hills Estate, his hands held a large pizza in a Dominoes box. "I made dinner," he said.

The pride in his voice was similar to that of my Jewish mother, who prepared dinner for my father every night for forty years. On a night off, ordering in takeout, she joked, "Well, I didn't *make* dinner, but I made it possible."

I smiled at Dr. Mohammad, "You sound like my mother."

In the hallway, Hala ran into me, pointing her finger and shouting, "Doesn't this one look like a terrorist?" A file containing high school transcripts, immunization records, and checking account numbers was being waved around wildly in the air. In the top corner was a student's name, written with a black Sharpie, next to a passport-sized photo stapled on, putting a name to the face of the student. Eyes peered out from a dark face covered in a traditional headdress. The image revealed few features, which were concealed by a full, thick, black beard, one that would make a thirty-year-old hipster envious.

"I'm so over how everyone talks around here," I dropped into the chair in Ashley's office, handing off a completed file. While I wanted to discuss morality and voice the downfalls of privilege that can come from the color of our skin, she was focused on camouflaging hers. Like a chameleon, her layer shed into the skin of a lawyer. "As you know, the Department of Homeland Security deems our office foreign soil, and in that regard, we do not abide by American labor laws."

Can we be on foreign soil and not be racist?

"I have someone in my extended family who is gay...I'm sure you can imagine how I feel."

Being private about my religion was one thing, but not speaking up for others was against everything I believed in. I needed to draw a line—the same one that she was trying to obscure. Thinking about this middle eastern country that was handing out opportunities to thousands of students, sending their future leaders to the US to broaden their minds, and yet, here I stood next to an American, explaining that when doors were open for business, the minds inside could be closed.

Leaving my disagreement with Ashley, a sound of excitement echoed into the hallway. I poked my head into the front office to see what the frenzy was about, wishfully thinking it meant freshly baked goods. "Oh, he'll get stopped, for sure," Hala laughed along with the other Arab divorcées, passing around a student file opened to the bio page with the passport photo stapled in front.

Glancing at the image, I saw an innocent looking eighteen-year-old boy along with his college applications. I imagined a young student, about to embark on his freshman year, arriving in the US, looking out the window of the plane filled with anticipation for the incredible journey ahead, only to be stopped at the airport, uncertain as to why he was pulled aside, detained in customs, trapped in purgatory away from his family, now having to defend himself in a foreign language to the guards—his welcome to the country he was only visiting. He would be considered one of the "lucky" ones.

When another student ended up in jail, he begged desperately, "Let them deport me. Just get me out of here!" The student shouted in Arabic to Dr. Mohammad through a wall that could not be broken. "Get me out of here."

"Inshallah *habibi*, inshallah, inshallah," Dr. Mohammad responded on his undiplomatic visit to the Los Angeles County Jail. He tried to convince the student and himself that they could navigate this. With no one to shine the light on what was ahead of him or how to get out, they were both left in the dark. The only familiar things surrounding him were his own thoughts, which were in a language no one around could decipher.

"I will die here," he shouted in Arabic. "The things they will do to me. I am just a boy amongst villains."

Dr. Mohammad hoped to give the student some reassurance but came back to the office looking like he saw a ghost. The fluorescent lights in the hallway highlighted his pale face and balding head. His once slim figure appeared as a frail body, his belt buckled on the very last hole, cinching his pants to hold them up. A clock ticked in the background, counting down the minutes visiting the student. Looking into a one-way mirror at the young man allowed Dr. Mohammad to see time running against him. The reflection showed a man he barely recognized—in his own prison, trapped in an office, chained to his desk without food, only seeing darkness as he arrived before the sunrise and leaving after sunset.

"He stands all alone, the poor, poor boy," Dr. Mohammad recounted to me. "No light, no window."

"He's okay, Dr. Mohammad."

"But there's nothing there," he explained.

"Dr. Mohammad, he's okay," I repeated, hoping to get him out of his trance.

"He waits alone," he repeated in the hallway, his gaze beyond my eyes. Standing by his side, listening to him repeat himself. "Complete darkness," Dr. Mohammad shuttered, recounting the visitation. "It's just so sad," he explained, "the student stopped by the police. Drunk driving." The student, who had already received multiple DUIs, also neglected to follow the US requirements for appearing in court.

"He's so lucky," I said, sighing with relief, hoping to shake Dr. Mohammad out of his trance.

"Ugh, the poor, poor guy, inshallah, he gets out soon," he exhaled.

"The student is so lucky," I repeated deliberately, shaking Dr. Mohammad out of his rumination long enough to glance towards me. "He's so lucky he went to jail." I paused long enough for Dr. Mohammad to digest what I was saying. "The student *is* blessed," I explained. "He could have hurt himself or worse, he could have hit and killed someone else's family." In a hushed voice, I repeated, "How lucky of the student to merely be in jail."

The irony was lost on me when I spoke my final words that day before leaving for San Diego. "We will all be okay," I said to Dr. Mohammad.

★ ★ ★

"I'm sorry," Leah said, opening the front door to the house that I should have been living in when Tyrone jumped out to stop her.

"Wait. Wait," he yelled. Both of them fought to get their words out first. "Look, Jess," Tyrone said, diverting my eyes to him.

"I've met someone," Leah said, bringing my attention back to her.

"Look, Jess," Tyrone said.

"Time to move out," Leah interjected.

While not even married for a year, Tyrone and I had been together for almost ten years. He held my hand through it all. Long before there were rings on our fingers, he stood by me in sickness and health. My courage to branch out stemmed from the foundation of his stability. His love breathed life into me time and time again. I believed our souls were intertwined.

As for the physical self, I knew every freckle on his face, the number of hairs he had above his lip resembling a prepubescent boy, and the almond shape of his eyes. I knew every muscle on his face—and was surprised that my stomach sank when I could tell he was hiding something through his grin.

Yet, for the first time since I moved to LA, I finally felt like I was capable of steadying myself. Managing the train ride to San Diego without taking a sedative allowed me to see life as it should be. I saw clearly.

"Leah first," I said.

Leah looked at Tyrone, for an okay, and looked back at me. "I hate saying this," she said, "I feel so bad. I just..." My eyes squinted trying to make sense of her words. "I hate doing this. His name is Brian. We're moving in together."

"My turn," Tyrone interjected. "Look," he said, pointing my eyes to the side of the porch. Leaning up against the fence, next to Tyrone's bike, was a rusted blue Schwimmer. "I made it for you," he said. "Been working on it a while. It kept me down here a little more than I would have liked, but..." he trailed off.

The life Tyrone and I were building was together, just not always in the same city. It didn't always make sense to others, the hours on the train and in the car, spending more time commuting only to steal a moment together. But it made sense to us. We were on a journey that didn't make sense to others, our path was clear, our love unwavering.

"So people hear you comin'." He honked the clown horn he put on the handlebars.

There was so much to celebrate beyond the Fourth of July. The long weekend meant only one of us would have to do the four-hour commute, with two days free in between without having to go in any direction. Time always ran against us with schedules that weren't our own to dictate, but the moment we were together, it stood still.

It was only the third of July, but energy filled the streets as a reminder that today, like any day, was a reason to celebrate. Taking advantage of the sun, the bikes, and the hours of freedom, we headed out to tour around with friends on Coronado, where even the seagulls are all white on the island known for its exclusivity. The quaint beach town was dressed up for the holiday, adding red and blue to its repertoire.

While locals rode around on beach cruisers, Tyrone and I joined friends for a pub crawl on our refurbished bikes. On the side of the road, my foot on the curb held me up on my bike, perching next to a college kid in his Cornell sweatshirt blasting the air conditioning of his Audi convertible with the top down. In the palm of his hand, he held the keys that opened more doors than a typical family on Coronado, with three garage spaces and a Cadillac golf cart parked in the driveway.

Stopping in at a bar, Tyrone waited to be served while standing next to a female navy cadet. She took a swig from a bottle of O'Doul's, sitting in silence, surrounded by the shouting of her peers. The male cadets cheered, "Shot, shot, shot, shot, shot, shot." Clinking their shot glasses together, they took the clear liquid down in one gulp, slamming them on the bar and then chasing them with a beer, hoping the ladies would be impressed by the mere sight of a man in uniform.

Tyrone brought me a glass of water on the busy patio of the pub with stunning views of white sails that regularly raced in regattas across the blue waters. A man in a Tommy Bahamas shirt, taking pictures to try to capture the beauty of the moment, asked the woman next to him, "Wouldn't you love to live here?"

I smirked at Tyrone. Both of us, knowing San Diego's history excluded Jews and Blacks from buying homes in neighborhoods like Coronado, "the Crown," and La Jolla, "the Jewel," so others wouldn't feel robbed of their privilege.

"Wasn't that a long time ago?" a friend asked.

"Is the '80s that long ago?" I replied, laughing to lighten the mood, knowing the topic made others uncomfortable, not light enough for discussion, but there was nothing funny about it.

Eventually, I would realize "No Jews allowed" was closer to home than the workplace. The office was deemed Kuwaiti soil, exempt from American Labor Laws, and was the first and only place to give me a chance. When I didn't believe in myself, Dr. Mohammad had faith in me. No other job came with that kind of offer.

Done with the island life, we headed back to reality before sunset, catching a ferry ride returning to the mainland. Like clockwork, the festivities started early in downtown San Diego, where Tyrone and I walked our bikes on the sidewalk, bustling with people bouncing in and out of the shops, restaurants, and bars.

In anticipation of the holiday, people who couldn't wait to shoot off fireworks started a night early, filling the air with smoke and echoing the startling "pop" sound, with helicopters above circling for the evening traffic report. Standing at the crosswalk, I stared at the traffic signal as a distraction from the loud noises that swirled around us. Tyrone and I waited for the light to change. A cue from the yellow box on the light post, cueing the pedestrians, resembled a Lite-Brite, with red pegs in the formation of a red hand to stop. The pegs would change to light up a white man on the traffic signal. He would let us know when we were safe to walk across the street.

Tyrone stepped forward off the curb, my foot pulled back, the shoelace caught on the gear. I kneeled down to release myself from the tangle, relieved that I uncharacteristically caught myself before falling. The soft cloth of the shoelace against my fingers contrasted with the poking of the metal chainring, the warmth of the summer evening against the cold concrete pressing against my opposite knee, holding my body steady. I retied the laces, my hands covered in the black lubricant that gives life and movement to the chain. An engine revved up to speed through the stoplight, rattling my eardrums and shaking the ground. The smell of the burning rubber was easier to swallow than the cloud emitted from the exhaust pipe. Forced into my lungs, I choked on the smoke, turning my head to catch my breath in a gasp for air. *Clink*. I heard the sound of a car hitting a tin can, knocked out of its way. *Clank*. The smoke cleared, as fast as the car drove off, jolting my body when I saw there was no tin can. Tyrone was lying in the middle of the crosswalk.

★ ★ ★

"L'chaim!" the guests shouted at our wedding after Tyrone stomped his foot on the traditional glass, shattering it with one strike as the rabbi chanted, "May your bond of love be as difficult to break as it would be to put back together these pieces of glass."

The shards of glass were strewn across the dirt path at the end of the aisle where Tyrone stood. Everyone we loved would be there, encircling us in prayer. It would only take one stomp to shatter. I cringed at the sound, hoping the glass wouldn't cut through Tyrone's shoe, slashing his skin open, blood seeping into his dress shoes, leaving a scar from our wedding day marked on his body. Everyone watched as I held his hand, reminding him that I was always there, but discreetly, I rubbed my thumb underneath his palm, awakening his senses to note my love was just for him to feel. It only took one blow to show how even with the strongest of bonds, a life of love can shatter into pieces in an instant.

★ ★ ★

Tyrone's body laid in the middle of the crosswalk in the dark of the night when a light turned green, cueing cars coming from the other direction to go. I ran into the middle of the road, holding my arm out, praying my body could stop the force of the oncoming traffic, while Tyrone used every ounce of adrenaline, fighting to drag his own body off the ground. In the darkness, I could see his collarbone looked like a broken wire hanger, now at a ninety-degree angle, protruding through his skin, which wasn't as alarming as the sound of him choking for air. I blinked, and in that time, Tyrone had been hit by a car, presumably by a drunk driver, who didn't stop to assess the damage.

I stared at Tyrone's chest, making sure it continued to rise each time it collapsed, as he choked on each breath, gurgling on the blood filling in his lungs. "Call 911," I shrieked at a nearby bouncer, gagging on the vomit that rose to my mouth, after rushing to Tyrone to ensure that his heart was still beating.

"Call 911," I yelled again.

"No, don't," a man interjected, "you'll pay for it later."

"Dude, they need a police report," the bouncer said.

"I'll get you a ride" was the last thing I heard.

Focused on Tyrone, I only listened to the sound of his breathing. I could no longer hear horns honking, people yelling, or music blasting from open car windows. I held my breath as I stared at Tyrone's chest, forcing it with my eyes to lift each time after it collapsed. When a rusty car pulled up to the corner, I didn't know how much time passed. Tyrone's body collapsed into the vinyl of the seat in the two-door vehicle. I rolled the window down on the passenger side before racing to the driver side to squeeze myself into the backseat. The wind smacked against the car, muting the sound of the gurgling in Tyrone's lungs. Unable to see him, I sat in darkness, praying the breeze coming in through the window pushed enough air into his lungs.

While the ambulances rushed other people in, Tyrone wrapped his arms around himself, trying to keep his body upright in a plastic seat in an empty waiting room, not saying a word. Meanwhile, I banged on the plastic barrier, begging the attendant behind it to help us. Chewing away at her gum, she pointed to a clipboard with four pages of questions to answer. The clock on the wall ticked louder and louder, like a bomb ready to go off, while the woman clicked her acrylic nails on her empty desk, counting down the minutes that I could last without exploding. Handing her the form I rushed to complete, I begged, "Please, help. Please." She scanned the pages, skipping through my notes, turning her gaze towards Tyrone to assess the damages by looking him over. "You filed a police report yet?" she asked.

"Beep," her cell phone interrupted. "Sorry," she said, shrugging her shoulders, her eyes and hand now locked on her phone, smiling as she sat comfortably in her chair, replying to a text message.

The waiting room felt like a dream once we were finally on the inside of the emergency room, packed with trauma, looking like an infirmary in a war zone, filled with people leaking blood all over their patriotic attire.

Tyrone lay on a hospital bed in the hallway as people rushed back and forth around us. "I'm okay," he whispered to comfort me as if he could shake this off. His words set off the fireworks as I burst into tears. The nurses rushed over, asking, "Are you alright?" But they weren't looking at Tyrone.

"Am *I* okay?" I snapped back at them, wondering, *Am I okay?*

A pale-faced resident in an oversized white lab coat interrupted my thoughts, using two hands to jerk the clipboard out from the end of Tyrone's bed. Scratching the pen on the paper, trying to get the ink to come out, the nurse's eyes lit up when she saw the doctor struggling, handing him a pen from her pocket. *Click. Click. Click.* The resident pushed on the pen incessantly. Staring at the clipboard, his cheeks blushed, without looking at us. The nurse handed off paperwork detailing every one of her assessments.

"Aww," the doctor said, staring down at her work. "Looks like a broken collarbone." Confirming what we could all see, the bone protruded like a wire hanger sticking out of his shoulder.

"We're going to send you home with some pain meds. Try to get some rest," he said. "Not much else we can do here."

Before we were discharged, a nurse brought the first dose of oxycontin, the controlled substance I would need to pick up at the sketchy CVS by the hospital, my usual spot for my own meds. I was well acquainted with the quickest path to the pharmacy as well as its obstacles. I knew to sprint from the parking lot up the stairwell, through the electric doors to avoid being accosted by the panhandler that blocked the handicap access ramp with his pit bull on a thick leash that nearly tripped me up every time. Tyrone could neither put the pill in his mouth nor tilt his head back to swallow it. Trying to avoid making any movement that would be too jarring, he used every muscle on the tip of his tongue to navigate the pill down his dry throat. Any relief of taking it was thwarted by the fear of what anguish vomiting it up might cause.

The pain from the hospital didn't dissipate with the scribbled note for the heavy narcotic. Leaving the hospital was scarier than heading there, knowing there was no relief ahead. The ride home from the hospital at two a.m. was silent. The only noise came out as a grunt from Tyrone clenching his teeth any time we hit a pebble in the road. His eyes were closed tightly, but I could see the pain, out of the corner of his lids, through the creases in his skin from wincing. There was no comfort in sight.

In the dark of the night, Tyrone stood backward, inching his bottom onto the bed, unable to lift his legs. He clenched tight to the headboard with his good hand. His ankles rested in the palm of my hands as I gradually raised them inch by inch until they were on the bed. Sitting upright, his polo was splashed with blood, grease, and dirt, cut open where his collar bone pushed his skin out like a tent. He cringed at the softness of the bed. "I'm okay," he whispered, without moving his lips to speak, in a voice I didn't recognize, muffled by the gurgling noise coming from his chest and the gagging sound of him choking on every breath. I delicately laid a blanket over his khaki pants, still neatly rolled up on one side, keeping it from snagging on the greasy chain on his bike. His shoes, laces still tied, looked heavy on his feet. His jaw clenched from the weight of the soft cotton barely touching his lower body. Every movement had a ripple effect on his face. His eyelids closed, a line drawn out from the corner, in the crease of his skin that grew deeper, cringing for the pain pulsing through his body, sending a twinge from even the blink of an eye.

I lifted an armchair up next to the bed without letting its feet touch the ground. Sitting upright, I stared at his chest, my contact lens sticking to my pupils. I felt a surge of guilt every time I blinked to relieve the dryness. Each gurgling noise coming from his mouth confirmed a breath. Then a pause. Followed by a gasp for air.

Chapter 24

Don't Miss A Beat

"You're gonna need to come back to the hospital," the voice of the triage nurse came through the line at four o'clock in the morning, two hours after we had made it home. "Now!"

After checking back in at the front desk of the emergency room, four nurses rushed out from behind closed doors, laying Tyrone on a medical bed, wheeling his body through the busy hallway of the hospital we had just left hours earlier. Like synchronized swimmers, they swirled around him in a fluid manner, showing an artistry of precision while performing with grace under pressure, making the exceptional work look routine. While taking all of his vitals, counting every breath, I held mine.

When a fresh-faced doctor arrived at the foot of the bed, the nurses dispersed as fluidly as they came together, rushing to care for the patients that flooded the space.

"He's likely having trouble breathing. Pulmonary contusion. His lungs are bruised pretty bad," the doctor said, looking at me, while Tyrone clenched his body, still holding it together, choking on the blood filling in his lungs. I held my breath, listening intently to the gurgling noise in Tyrone's throat.

The well-rested radiologist on the morning shift, reviewing the charts from the previous night, noticed what had been overlooked hours before.

"You can see the obvious broken collar bone," he said. "Unfortunately, we missed the nine broken ribs. Total slipup."

A shrill scream echoed loudly inside my head; I cupped my hands to my ears to escape the sound of my thoughts, bursting into tears, cuing the doctor to ask, "Are you alright?" But he wasn't looking at Tyrone.

The words ignited a flame, boiling the blood inside my body. "Am *I* okay?" I fumed. "A slipup?" My mind didn't have time to add up every moment that mattered. While Tyrone's life weighed in the hands of others, I stood on the solid ground that he helped pave, shouldering the burden of my anxiety with his unwavering love, letting me know *I* was safe.

The sound of sirens in the background signaled an ambulance on approach. Louder and louder, the next emergency was getting closer, threatening our relevance. My imperceptible voice felt like striking a match and throwing it into a dormant volcano. Friction unsettled the layers, flaming the fire, deep within, igniting the eruption. "Is this how you care for a Black man?" The words came out like hot lava, scorching anyone near, stopping the nurses in their tracks.

The doctor looked at Tyrone and then looked at me. His shoulders shrugged with his hands up in the air. "It's my third day," he said, hands trembling. In the ER, where seconds mattered, we learned, residents across the nation started on the first of July. The young man who stood in front of us, with patients' lives in his hands, had only been called a doctor for the last three days. His oversized scrubs now stood out, draping over his body, the sound of the pen against the clipboard rattled. He now resembled a child, afraid to look me in the eyes when he said, "He's going to need surgery."

Chapter 25

Picking Up The Pieces

"Tyrone, hit by car," I texted Dr. Mohammad. "Not returning to work." Without time to wrap my head around anything beyond each minute ahead of me, I left Dr. Mohammad to fill in the blanks. Saying so little, he would still get the message.

Looking for something to heal Tyrone, I stood in the kitchen, staring into the pantry, wishing a box of brownie mix sat on the shelf to ease my pain. Instead, I found a can of chicken soup to warm up over the stove. Waiting for the small pot to boil, I glanced at the empty screen of the phone, wondering if Dr. Mohammad saw my text.

Unable to raise a spoon to his mouth, Tyrone would need to slurp the soup without moving his arms. I got down on my hands and knees to search through the cabinet for a lobster pot. In the deepest corner of the shelf, covered in dust, was the wedding gift that was never touched by a crustacean of any kind. After wiping it off, I flipped it upside down and placed it on the dining room table, on top of a stack of yellow pages pulled from the recycling bin. I turned my head towards the sound of Tyrone's slippers sliding inch by inch along the hardwood floors. Without peeking my head out, creating un-solicited attention, I waited without moving an inch, listening intently to verify the sound of a stool pulled out from under the dining room table, confirming he made it. Avoiding the crunch of his ribs by sitting in a chair, Tyrone slid his body onto the barstool.

The flames from the gas stove flickered brightly as the soup boiled out of the pot, dripping over the sides, igniting a larger flame. Unfazed by the fire, I propped a window open, keeping the sensitive smoke detector from going off. A fire alarm outside of my mind would be too much of a disruption.

A large ladle scooped the steaming soup into the bowl, which was then carefully placed on top of the lobster pot on top of the yellow pages, which created a tower that met at the level of Tyrone's mouth. A balancing act of sorts. Far above the table, at a height that kept his body as close to a straight angle as possible.

"I could've done that," Tyrone said. I couldn't imagine which part of it he believed he could do. He was barely able to balance his body from making anything more than a slight motion.

"Of course," I replied.

An oversized bag of dirty laundry and a stack of quarters followed me in tow to the washer and dryer behind the house. I threw the pile of soiled clothes into the grimy machine, hop-ing to wash away the memories of the accident, wondering if the rusted device that looked dirtier than the blood-stained clothes would be able to do its job. My six quarters jammed into the slots that the landlord hacked on to the side. The jittering of the coins falling chimed through, ringing like the joyful sounds of the slot machines in Vegas. But I knew that in reality, we already pushed our luck. The machine rumbled as a warm-up before spinning the clothes to balance the load. My eyes stared blankly, hoping the rhythm would hypnotize my thoughts.

The sound of dishes breaking from inside the house snapped me back to the kitchen where Tyrone's head was down, vomiting into the lobster pot. After only taking a few sips of the soup, bile spewed out of his mouth like a volcano. He pulled a breath into his lungs to say, "In my pants." The words triggered his body to heave into the pot again on his breath out. He took a breath in to say, "Get in my pants." Choking on his words, he vomited again on his exhale. With his head deep inside the lobster pot, he could still feel my questioning stare, responding, "Get prescription. Pants pocket."

The suds cycle locked the clothes in from the outside. The water and soap swished around, taunting while the locked door refused to open. I slipped my arm behind the back of the machine, feeling the heat emanate off the metal. Wishing not to touch it, my eyes closed tight to pull the cord out of the socket. Even without power, the force from the machine continued to spin. As if slowing down a ceiling fan with a hand, I reached in, desperate to get the soiled pants out of the soap.

A feeling of relief washed over my body when I saw a light blue color peeking out of the brown khakis that looked like they were the star of a foam party in Ibiza, drenched in suds and bubbles. To save the drenched paper from falling apart in the palm of my hand, I pushed the pocket out from the inside of the pants. The bloodstains left their mark, but the blue ink washed off the remnants of paper that no longer resembled a prescription for the narcotic.

"Bing," sounded from my cell phone, redirecting me back to the kitchen. The text from Dr. Mohammad read, "Inshallah, he's okay." The words fused with my thoughts, whirling around with so much force, there was no way to escape as it swallowed me whole, forcing me to feel its power. "Inshallah." Dr. Mohammad wrote again, at the bottom of his text, "You will be okay."

★ ★ ★

Even when we lived hundreds of miles apart, Tyrone never left my side. Every step of the way, he was there, picking me up off the floor when I was a puddle to raise me up in strength. Believing each time I would get myself back together. His love created a life vest, keeping me afloat, allowing me to test the waters in the deep end. Every time I dove in headfirst with my eyes closed, I knew he wouldn't let me drown. Feeling wobbly, I now needed to be the stable one.

★ ★ ★

Without asking any questions, Dr. Mohammad made sure all of my work was covered. Not a single email or phone call would interrupt the time he afforded me to stay where I most wanted to be. In the moments I pretended not to be consumed with Tyrone's every move, I was thinking about the economic crisis that led me to LA in the first place. In 2009, Americans who lost health insurance were at risk of losing everything. It was evidence for too many, including President Obama, how one accident or one illness without health insurance could bankrupt a family. There was too much at stake. As the days went by in San Diego, I watched Tyrone rest. Little by little, his cheeks regained their rosy red coloring, his freckles lit up with a small grin. When he tired of me watching him, I knew it was time to get back to work.

When the alarm went off at 6 a.m., three weeks after the accident, the sound echoed in the bare studio apartment in LA on the corner of the busy street. No photos, pictures, or posters made their way onto the barren walls. Getting up from the futon, I took the sheets off and threw them into a ball, stuffing them into the closet, then converting the bed back into a couch, where I would sit alone after returning from work. The water in the shower ran through a labyrinth of old pipes to heat up as I stood naked on the cold tile floor, pained by the sound of the water wasting away, using less time to rinse off than it took for the water to warm up.

After drying off, I unwrapped the towel from my body to wipe off the steam from the antique beveled mirror that framed my face in the dimly lit hall. I sat with my makeup bag at the built in vanity I never used. Tracing the red lipstick around my mouth, my reflection was almost gray, aging my face, giving me a glimpse of both my current and future state. The aged mirror, too small to show my full reflection, only offered a glimpse of each part of me. Treading lightly on the hardwood floor, I inched backward for a better view, but the vision was blurred, unable to capture what I wanted to see.

At the Kuwaiti Cultural Office, nothing changed. As if saying, "Hi," my coworkers asked, "How's Tyrone?" But after everyone made their rounds, work drudged on, as always.

Endless emails filled the week with students' "urgent" requests that didn't seem to matter anymore.

"Don't leave me," Liz said.

"I'm just going back for the weekend."

She narrowed her eyebrows at me.

While I was just trying to get through the days, she was looking ahead. When I skipped lunch saying, "I'm so behind. Just trying to get caught up," she knew I didn't want to get ahead. I wanted to be on the train, heading home to San Diego to be with Tyrone. I missed the life I wanted to be living.

The Friday of the first week away from Tyrone after the accident was the only time in nearly two years that the train left the station without me. It departed ten minutes before I arrived, leaving me alone on a bench in Union Station, waiting hours for the next one.

During rush hour at the start of the weekend, the crowds scrambled, shoving their way through, trying to get ahead, not caring who got bumped along the way. When the clock tower chimed, it overpowered the whizzing of the chaos, the bells ringing as a reminder that even when we sit still, time moves faster than the train, not stopping in its tracks to wait for anyone.

Chapter 26

When Opportunity Knocks, Answer The Door

"I'm worried you'd be bored here," a woman dressed in jeans and a t-shirt with laced up sneakers said while looking over my resume. It was eighty degrees in San Diego, and I was wearing an all-black, freshly dry-cleaned, business suit, a white collared blouse, and pearl earrings. In October of 2010, three months after the accident, Tyrone and I celebrated one year of marriage. There was no traffic on the ten-minute drive from the house, which left me sitting in the car for an hour in the parking lot of the university campus. No security guards or valet waited outside holding the door ajar to a Mercedes-Benz idling out front. My Honda blended in.

I sat on the edge of a narrow bench across from the student assistant working the front desk in her half top and cut offs. Texting away on her cell phone, she looked up from time to time to find someone politely waiting for her to notice them. Her long brown hair and bright pink lipstick dissuaded her audience from being impatient.

When the director of the university's international student center arrived, she tossed her brown paper lunch bag into the overflowing trash bin, which propped the front door of the office open. Reaching her hand out to shake mine, I stared down, keeping my hands by my sides.

Squinting her eyes, unsure of what was happening, she waved her hand away from the awkward encounter, saying, "Come on back."

A north window of the director office looked right into the parking lot where the meter maids circled. The dusty blinds were crooked and drawn halfway down the window to limit the light from shining on the computer screen that leaned against the tower.

"Don't mind the chaos," she said, catching my glimpse at the student files spread out all over the floor. "Haven't had time yet. Just settling into my new office," she grinned.

"Did HR explain our situation?" The director continued without pausing, "We are looking for a temporary advisor. Three months. Not sure beyond that. Desperate to have someone start right away." She looked me straight in the eye to see if I appeared turned off. I stared back, unfazed by her words.

The associate director knocked on the closed door, waiting for permission to enter. The two women sat staring at my resume, not knowing where to start.

"Why would you want to work here?" the associate director asked, giving her time to study my resume as if seeing it for the first time. The answer I wouldn't share didn't matter to them, so instead, I told them what I knew they wanted to hear.

"I see you work for Dr. Mohammad," the director chimed in. "Very impressive." His name said it all. Like the Kuwaiti crest on every memo, working for him was the stamp of approval. "Anyone that's worked for him should work for me."

"Wouldn't you'd be bored here?" the associate director interjected, cueing the director to click her tongue in annoyance, striking it from the record. I smiled back, knowing boredom was something I could endure for a ten-minute commute to the life I waited years to live.

A few weeks later, the human resources manager for the university called to offer the position of "emergency hire." Three months of work, only a possibility of extending, for nearly half my current salary and two and a half hours of vacation time accrued every month. "And you would have to pay for parking." I heard all I needed to hear, and then her voice whispered through the phone, "I wouldn't take it if I were you."

★   ★   ★

"You're pregnant," Dr. Mohammad announced in his office, slipping me a folded piece of paper across his desk as I stood across from him, staring at the blue skies that surrounded his office.

"No, Dr. Mohammad. I'm not pregnant."

He sighed with great relief, relaxing back in his chair.

Moments earlier, when he heard me announce, "I have news" without a caseload in my arms, he replied with a gasp, "I'll write it down."

"Okay?" I replied, unfamiliar with the game he thought I was playing.

He explained, "I will write on a piece of paper what I think you are about to tell me. Then I will pass it to you. Like a magic trick." He scribbled on a piece of paper, the palm of his hand cupped around it, hiding what card he was going to play. He pushed it forward face down on the desk. I waited for him to leave the paper in front of me, ensuring our hands wouldn't meet at the same time, but before I was able to open the piece of paper, he blurted out, "You're pregnant!"

I shook my head. "I'm gonna go work in San Diego." I paused, allowing the words to sink in, as he filled in the blanks. There was no need to explain the details. That wasn't what mattered to either of us. These were the cards dealt.

"The rains go everywhere," he replied in proverb. The red in his face became darker, yet what stood out were the deep creases at the corner of his eyes and just below, the even darker circles.

The once empty space, where we sat on the floor to celebrate my nuptials, was now filled with cubicles and a staff of employees to fill every new seat.

"The storm has passed," I replied. "Look at what you've done."

"You've made a mistake," he said, looking past me to see what the other advisors were up to beyond his office door. "Yes, you can go be under your husband's umbrella. But this here," he paused, "*we* have done."

★ ★ ★

Four weeks later, my transition to SDSU was easier for Dr. Mohammad than it was for me. My new role, advising international students sponsored by foreign government scholarships, made it my responsibility to take care of Dr. Mohammad from the university side.

Liz and I had less time for our catch up, but we checked in daily. "Your replacement is already going on vacation," she chuckled, over the phone. "She requested two weeks off."

"How is that possible?" I responded to Liz. Even over the phone, Liz could see the look on my face. We were each other's sounding boards for two years, starting within days of each other, working endless hours, establishing the ground-work for those who would come long after us. She knew how hard it was to work there, but even more so, she knew how much harder it was for me to leave.

"Jess," she shouted, interrupting my thoughts. "She asked for two weeks off...to go to Israel. She's Jewish."

I tried to keep up with my racing thoughts, putting all the pieces together. I heard the voice that said, "Jews can't work here." It was Fatema's. When she was fired, it was a shock to the office. We all believed an Arabic-speaking Muslim with an MBA from Stanford was an ideal employee. "She's not who I thought she was," Dr. Mohammad had said leaving us confused with his explanation. "He who digs a pit for his brother, falls into it." I pictured Dr. Mohammad sitting behind his grand mahogany desk, covered in official government documents, student files stacked high, with his back to the floor to ceiling windows, offering his staff the perspective, a 180-degree view of the city of stars. While he was able to see the path right ahead, he saw Fatema was trying to keep people out, and this went against one of the first rules I learned working for him: "The doors remain open for all to pass through."

★ ★ ★

When my phone rang at ten o'clock that evening, I recognized the number and knew my job wasn't on the line. It was Dr. Mohammad's US cell phone. A thrill in his voice came through when he called asking for help for a student, a question that any advisor in the office could have easily answered.

Regardless of my job, he knew he could call on me. There was no longer static or difficulty hearing what was unsaid; nothing was lost in translation. "*Shukran*," he said, thanking me for my help in the matter, "*Shukran, habibti,* you have always been who I knew you could be."

Chapter 27

Cutting The Cord

"We are thinking of naming the baby Mona," I said over the phone to Dr. Mohammad in January 2012.

"MOH-nah," Dr. Mohammad said slowly to make sure he pronounced it correctly, then repeated to himself, "MOH-nah. That is wonderful!" he exclaimed with such excitement I wondered if it were the name of one of his daughters. "MOH-nah, like MOH, as in Dr. Mohammad. Now, every time you say her name, you will think of Dr. Mohammad."

February 17, 2012, fourteen months after starting my job in San Diego, I gave birth to a baby girl. Dr. Mohammad received the birth announcement in the mail, a black and white photo of her little body tucked into Tyrone's arm. Her eyes wide open, beaming with such intensity they'd burn a hole through your body, to completely melt your heart. In a delicate yet bold font was her name, Ahuvah Orli, and the Jewish quote, "All our love every day; every day with our love," just as it had been in Hebrew on our wedding invitation. I pictured Dr. Mohammad opening the envelope in a vision I saw so clearly. Ahuvah would stare straight back at him as he held the delicate card in his hands, bringing it closer to his eyes to take it all in, and at that moment, they would see eye to eye.

In October 2012, eight months after giving birth, I texted Dr. Mohammad. "I'm in the neighborhood. Can I drop by for a minute?" Tyrone, Ahuvah, and I were headed to Los Angeles for sixteen hours of international flights to the island of Sardinia to attend a wedding. This union would bring together old friends in good health to celebrate what mattered most. Just getting to LA was a trip, stopping to nurse, change diapers, and soothe the baby, all while fighting bumper to bumper traffic. But this adventure was the one I most wanted to be on, with my love, after sickness and now in health.

"Wait. You didn't ask him in advance?" Tyrone said, choking on the realization.

"No, it's fine. That's just how it works with him."

Returning to the fancy glass entryway of the towering building, I was immediately stopped by the guards, who stood blocking the way to the lobby. Two years had passed since I worked for the Kuwaiti government. A security badge no longer demonstrated I was supposed to be there.

Three phone calls made by the security detail permitted us to enter the elevator as a guard used his security pass offering access to the eighteenth floor. One arm wrapped around Tyrone, a palm gripping his hand, and the other arm held the baby as we rode to the eighteenth floor together as a family.

Thinking I knew my place, we headed down the familiar hallway towards the two chairs that remained empty, opposite Dr. Mohammad. Charging towards us, like a bull, he shouted,

"La, la, la. No, no, no." Tyrone and I tried to step back, finding ourselves feeling cornered in his office. My body felt heat rising, sensing a change in the air. Dr. Mohammad stepped in closer to me than I ever thought was allowed. His voice amplified in Arabic while shaking his hand at us emphatically. Tyrone turned his glance towards mine, appearing uncharacteristically unnerved and uncertain, looking for a cue to see how to respond. Dr. Mohammad took us both by surprise, lunging at us.

"La, la, la," he yelled, swooping in, grabbing hold of the baby. "Sit, sit, sit," he said, directing us to a space I never sat in before. The relief of my exhausted body melted into the leather couch by the glass table that only sat high ranking guests, government officials, members of the royal family, and diplomats.

"A little candy?" the father of five offered to the eight-month-old baby, who was only nursing.

"Thank you, I'll save it for later," I said, putting the candy in my pocket.

"To keep the baby comfortable then…," he said, bouncing the baby, trailing off as he walked out of his office, parading her around.

The staff still paced like cougars in a corral, circling now, waiting for their moment to pounce, alarmed by the ringing sounds of the phones momentarily left unanswered. Dr. Mohammad reached into his pocket to pull out his phone, placing it on the desk of his assistant, who glanced at it like it was a ticking time bomb, not wanting to make physical contact or have anything to do with a phone left out, unanswered. "Take a photo," Dr. Mohammad directed to his assistant. "Ohhhhhh, goo goo goo *habibti*," Dr. Mohammad cooed, as he posed for a photo with Ahuvah in his arms, holding her up high like a trophy.

My heart was full, but my arms were empty. In the past eight months of sleepless nights, I stared at our first child, ensuring she never missed a breath. The soft leather couch absorbed the weight of my body, freeing my mind of any burden I experienced there before, allowing my eyes to play, gazing around the room. The view out of the floor to ceiling windows was something I never saw from that perspective. A traffic light on Sunset Boulevard shined green, allowing the cars to move forward across the expansive city that I navigated through.

"Please visit us again soon," he pleaded, gazing at Ahuvah. I was unsure if we would ever be back or see Dr. Mohammad again. His term only lasted one more year before he would be required to return home.

"Next time in Kuwait?" I suggested with a shrug.

Laughing, Dr. Mohammad and I looked toward each other and said, "Inshallah."

About the Author

Jessica Naomi Keith is a professor of cross-cultural communication at San Diego State University. She graduated from Occidental College and received her master's degree in international education from the University of San Francisco. She has worked for two foreign governments at the Embassy of Spain and The Consulate of Kuwait. A Community Action Grant from the American Association of University Women was awarded to her to produce her documentary, *Beyond Our Boundaries*, distributed by Berkely Media. She has been published in the *New York Times*, Kveller, McSweeney's, The Nosher, Scary Mommy, Uptown News, Sammiches & Psych Meds, PJ Library, Medium, and BLUNTmoms. Publications are chronicled at Jessica's website, www.jessicakeithwriter.com. Jessica lives in sunny San Diego with her soulmate and their three children, the family's first generation of Black Jews.